Whol

Roy Williamson is an Hono... ...~~istant~~ Bishop in the Diocese of Southwell and was previously Bishop of Bradford (1984–91) and Bishop of Southwark (1991–98). He was also Archdeacon of Nottingham and the incumbent of three parishes in that city. His previous books include *Can You Spare a Minute* and *For Such a Time as This* (published by DLT) and *Joyful Uncertainty*, *Open Return* and *Not Least in the Kingdom* (all SPCK). He is married with three sons, two daughters and seven grandchildren.

Wholly Alive

*Integrating Faith and
Everyday Life*

Roy Williamson

SPCK

Published in Great Britain in 2003
Society for Promoting Christian Knowledge
Holy Trinity Church
Marylebone Road
London NW1 4DU

Copyright © Roy Williamson 2003

All rights reserved. No part of this book may be reproduced or transmitted in any form or by any means, electronic or mechanical, including photocopying, recording, or by any information storage and retrieval system, without permission in writing from the publisher.

Scripture quotations from the New Revised Standard Version of the Bible are copyright © 1989 by the Division of Christian Education of the National Council of the Churches of Christ in the USA. Used by permission. All rights reserved.

British Library Cataloguing-in-Publication Data
A catalogue record for this book is available from the British Library

ISBN 0-281-05519-X

1 3 5 7 9 10 8 6 4 2

Typeset by FiSH Books, London WC1
Printed in Great Britain by Bookmarque Ltd, Croydon, Surrey

Contents

Acknowledgements		viii
Introduction		ix
1	Hands	1
2	Eyes	9
3	Mouth	16
4	Heart	24
5	Mind	33
6	Will	42
7	Friends, neighbours, enemies	50
8	Past	59
9	Present	68
10	Future	77
11	Death	86
12	Life	94
Epilogue		103
Anthology of Prayers		105
References		116

For
my sister
Molly

Acknowledgements

Once again I am grateful to my editor Alison Barr for her ready encouragement and helpful advice, and to Jean Cherry for reading the text and offering suggestions for improvement.

Unless otherwise stated, all biblical quotations are taken from the New Revised Standard Version.

I have altered, of course, the names and locations of the various people mentioned in order to preserve their identity.

Acknowledgements for the Anthology of Prayers are as follows:

David Adam, *The Edge of Glory*, SPCK, 1985.

John Baillie, reproduced from *The Oxford Book of Prayer*, edited by George Appleton (1985), by permission of Oxford University Press.

Michael Botting, in *The SPCK Book of Christian Prayer*, SPCK, 1995.

Margaret Cropper, reproduced by permission of Stainer & Bell Ltd, London, England.

Janet Morley, in *All Desires Known*, SPCK, 1992.

Reinhold Niebuhr, in *Hymns of Worship*, Association Press, New York, 1939.

John V Taylor, from *A Matter of Life and Death*, SCM Press, 1986, p. 49.

Introduction

Honesty may be the best policy but it can be painful, as I discovered on the night I called Edwin a 'spike'. He was organist at the church where I was a young, and relatively inexperienced, lay minister. He was high church and rather fond of ritual. I was considered low church and evangelical. But we became good friends and, being a bachelor, he frequently came to our home after choir practice to drink gallons of tea and munch mountains of toast with my wife and me, sometimes staying until the wee small hours.

It was during one such late night sitting that I, feeling that our friendship could survive a light-hearted 'honesty session', plucked up courage to ask him a personal question. 'Edwin', I said, 'I hope you'll forgive my raising the matter but people from my tradition often refer to a person like you as a "spike". You are so high up the candle that you have almost disappeared!'

'Now', I continued, swallowing hard, 'what do you call people like me?' He smiled, picked up another piece of toast and replied, 'Ah! well, since we're playing the honesty game, you are known as a "God-botherer". Evangelicals always appear to be bothering God with every little detail of life. They don't seem to be able to do anything without referring to the Almighty, asking for his help and expecting miracles every other day!'

To cover what I'm sure he felt would be an embarrassing silence, he reached for the teapot and began to pour. But he needn't have worried about my reaction. I was convulsed with laughter. His playful stereotyping was too close to the truth for comfort and the only way I could deal with it was to laugh at myself. And I'm glad I did, for it liberated me. It started me on a journey of self-discovery that set me free from an immature dependency on God and, instead, helped me towards a much larger and more biblical view of the creator and my relationship to him.

In the early days of my Christian life, I was thrilled at the thought that 'God was on my side'. I was in awe at the power that seemed available to me, and staggered by the knowledge that I could make my needs known to him and expect answers to my prayers. To be honest, I shudder as I recall some of the inappropriate attitudes I adopted towards God and the immature demands I made upon him. There were times, I fear, when I behaved as though he was at my 'beck and call', a divine 'Mr Fix it', who could be relied upon to intervene when things went wrong. Such was his amazing grace and generous understanding, however, that often he appeared to give me the things I desired and to sort out the people and problems causing me difficulty. It seemed that God, in his goodness and patience, recognized the enthusiasm of a new Christian, forgave the arrogance of immaturity, and gave me great encouragement in my new-found faith.

A framework for life

But as time moved on, I began to discover a deeper enthusiasm and more lasting encouragement in seeing God not as some kind of SAS commander who parachuted in to help me when I was at my wit's end, but rather as the sovereign creator 'in whom we live and move and have our being'. He was not someone who periodically intervened at my request, but one to whom I was intimately related and whose love for and care of me never ceased.

At that point, prayer stopped resembling a shopping list of my personal concerns and requirements. It ceased being simply a liturgical exercise or a special form of words. It became more a way of life: a close and continuing relationship with a God of love, of intimacy, of everlasting giving, sharing and receiving, which embraced every aspect of life and every part of my personality.

Of course, I continued to bring my needs to God, as Jesus

taught me to do (Matthew 6.7–13). And of course, I received answers to my prayers, as Jesus taught me to expect (Matthew 7.7–11). But my prayer became less of a request and more of an offering, less a reminding God of what was happening in his world and the way it was affecting me, and more a placing of myself and my concerns within the orbit of his loving providence and care.

Prayer had become the expression of my whole person: body, mind and spirit. It was not a private ethereal exercise unrelated to the people or the world around me. It was an offering of my whole self to God within the concrete relationships of this world, something I believe St Paul had in mind when he encouraged the Christians in Rome to 'present your bodies as a living sacrifice, holy and acceptable to God' (Romans 12.1).

It was with this thought of an offering of the whole person to God, within the network of our human relationships in the world, that I began to see prayer not only as a way of life but also as providing a framework for life. The deliberate daily offering of my whole self to God isn't an excuse for opting out of active involvement in the world, quite the reverse. It is a recognition that God never ceases to be at work in his world, and of the importance of placing myself at his disposal as a partner in that work. The offering to God of my hands and heart, my mind and will, my words and deeds, for instance, commits me to use those gifts responsibly in my relationships with others. My love for and gratitude to God, expressed in the prayerful offering of my whole self – body, mind and spirit – demands a practical outworking in love for my neighbour, justice for the oppressed and healing for the world in its brokenness. My love of neighbour reveals the reality of my love for God.

It is the basic framework for life spelt out by God in the Ten Commandments and lived out by Jesus during his time on earth. He loved God with all his heart and soul and mind and strength, and his neighbour – and his enemies – as himself. And he did so within the concrete relationships, frustrations, constraints and opportunities of everyday life.

This little book tries to provide a simple framework to enable us to follow his example. It does so by reflecting upon some of the human faculties we use, the relationships we share and issues we face every day. It makes no claim to be a sophisticated blueprint for successful Christian living. It is a humble offering that I hope will provide a sense of integration and purpose, support and inspiration, to all who are endeavouring to live the life of faith.

1
Hands

It is often said of demonstrative people, including many preachers, that they would be speechless without their hands. Most of us, however, would be useless without them. A minor injury to a thumb or forefinger tends to make the simplest task immensely difficult, if not impossible. The threading of a needle, the tying of a shoelace or the knotting of a tie becomes a major challenge, often ending in frustration and a cry for help!

Without the full use of our hands, our actions are severely limited. It is by the creative use of our hands that we do so many things and achieve so much. Every single day it is our hands that express our individual purposefulness, skill and uniqueness. That is true not only of the concert pianist, the heart surgeon or the physiotherapist, but also of the flower arranger, the home help and the copy-typist.

There are exceptions, of course, but what we do with our hands usually reveals not only the nature of our work, but also the priorities of our life. In the lives of most of us, it is the work of our hands that brings us a sense of identity and fulfilment. And that same work, creatively and devotedly done, can bring pleasure and inspiration to others.

A shining example

That was certainly true of Bernard in his professional life. He had been a silversmith for forty years. But then came retirement and with it, a temporary crisis of identity. There were no demands for his creative skills, no delight being expressed at the quality of his workmanship, no adrenalin flowing from the pressure to meet deadlines. Life was a bit flat and, despite his Christian faith, Bernard indulged in a little self-pity and had a quiet moan at God for removing him from the so-called fast lane and parking him in a lay-by.

But the crisis didn't last long. Bernard's extroverted personality reasserted itself. His smile and sense of humour returned and so did a balanced attitude to his prayers. I shall never forget his comments on the day he rang to tell me, excitedly, that he had a new job. Before he got round to the detail, he told me, with restored humour, that for weeks he had been 'playing silly beggars' with God. 'But thankfully', he said, 'God has sorted me out!'

Apparently, he had spent weeks bombarding God with all kinds of requests and suggestions as to what he thought the Almighty might do for him. But there didn't seem to be any answers. Almost in desperation, he changed the agenda and began to reflect that, perhaps, there was something he might be able to do for God. So, sitting quietly and prayerfully at home one morning, he thanked God for the creative skills he had been given during his professional life, and the pleasure this had brought to other people. Then, holding out his open hands, he offered them once more to God for use in whatever way he wanted.

It was a brave thing to do. For opening our hands to God implies not only that we are offering him all we have and are, but also that we are ready to accept whatever he may send to us.

And that, together with an appeal for help in the parish magazine, is how Bernard came to be the official shiner of brass and polisher of wood in his ancient parish church. For that was his new job – and it was no mean task, as he soon discovered. Thousands of visitors came to the church each year to view interesting and important memorials and take photographs of valuable pieces of furniture. The proper maintenance of these artefacts was an important witness to the wider community, and Bernard took it seriously. He brought the same dedication and purpose to this voluntary task as he had done to his professional career. And as a result, visitors were unanimous in their praise of the care which was being taken to preserve these particular church treasures, and many of them were inspired and encouraged in their own life of faith.

Bernard's initial excitement never cooled. Polishing church brass might be considered by some to be a rather mundane occupation. He saw it as a significant piece of work to be done for God.

Though our experience may differ greatly from Bernard's, his example has important implications for every one of us. Our hands, and all that they represent in terms of skill, creativity and service, must never be taken for granted. A better way is to offer them to God, and consciously to place our hands each day in his. By this simple and symbolic offering, we not only acknowledge our dependence upon God, but also our responsibility to use our talents in the service of others. Perhaps we do more, for in placing our hands in his, we make them, and every aspect of our daily life and work, available for him to use in whatever way he chooses. This can invest the humblest of activities with deep significance.

A divine touch

Such thinking is neither fanciful nor theoretical. It is both true and practical, and, if I may say so, breathtakingly exciting. For if we place our hands in his and do our work, whatever it may be, in his name, then it becomes an extension of our prayer of offering or oblation. In other words, it becomes part of our worship. It gives meaning and purpose to the most ordinary, even dreary, actions of our daily lives.

We could find this thought easier to accept, perhaps, if what we are doing carries a significance that is publicly recognized and clearly of value to the health and wholeness of the community. The skill of the surgeon saving lives, the concert pianist stirring the emotions, or the watercolour artist capturing the stunning beauty of spring blossom, are obvious examples.

But we mustn't be selective or place limits on what God is prepared to own and bless. That is his choice, not ours. What we may consider mundane he may wish to exalt and give it a significance beyond our imagining. Our Lord found eternal significance in the offering of a cup of cold water to the needy (Matthew 10.42). As George Herbert poetically pointed out in his famous hymn, 'Teach me my God and King', whatever the nature of the work of our hands, if done as an offering to God, it will have a touch of the divine about it.

> A servant with this clause
> Makes drudgery divine;
> Who sweeps a room, as for thy laws,
> Makes that and the action fine.

There are many ordinary activities of life that provide opportunity for a divine touch to rest upon the work of our hands.

To illustrate the point, I think of one such activity that is within the competence of every one of us, namely, the writing of personal letters or cards. It is an underused and undervalued gift from God. Of course, like other gifts it can be misused, leading to unnecessary hurt rather than help or healing. Letters containing vitriol, prejudice and verbal violence, whether they are anonymous or signed, do not have their origin in God. But there is little doubt that personal notes or letters, thoughtfully written and sensitively timed, can bring great joy and encouragement to people at significant moments in their lives.

Over the years I have been on the receiving end of scores of such letters and cards. Indeed, I have retained many of them and use them as bookmarks to remind me of those moments when God came alongside me in the words of a friend. Some are humorous, and at the time they were received served to 'take the mickey' out of me for some foolish comment or pompous act. Some are subtle and affirming, while others are sensitive and compassionate. All of them were timely. There was a sense that the writer, before putting pen to paper, had offered to God in prayer the particular context into which they were being sent. So often, therefore, they came with all the pertinence and power of a 'word from the Lord'. The classic one showed a lonely isolated cottage, above which a rainbow stood out across a dark, foreboding sky. To me, at the time, it carried the touch of the divine and spoke volumes to my circumstances.

The same can be true of every aspect of the work of our hands if offered to God. This was uniquely so in the life and work of Jesus Christ.

A unique offering

Jesus lived, died and rose again to glorify God. He didn't set out to make a name for himself, but to bring honour to his Father. Creating a distinctive lifestyle was not his primary concern. In all aspects of his life and work, he pointed to God and showed the way. His mission in life was to do the will of his Father (John 4.34). Nevertheless, God honoured him for his life of self-giving obedience, revealed his glory through him and gave him the name that is above every name (Philippians 2.5-11). Father and Son were bound together in a mutual sharing, giving and receiving in the power of the Spirit.

This was demonstrated at Jesus' baptism, when his dedication to the will of his Father was affirmed by the Father's testimony, and empowered by the Holy Spirit.

> And when Jesus had been baptized, just as he came up from the water, suddenly the heavens were opened to him and he saw the Spirit of God descending like a dove and alighting on him. And a voice from heaven said, 'This is my Son, the Beloved, with whom I am well pleased. (Matthew 3.16-17)

The incredibly purposeful life and work of Jesus was made possible by the power of God the Father and his own self-giving obedience. His life was offered to God unreservedly. He placed himself in the hands of his Father, and revealed his Father's character and purpose in the life he lived and the work he did. Friend and foe alike bore witness to his unique life. He spoke and the dead were raised to life. He laid his hands on the sick and they were healed. With a word of command he cast out demons. He took bread in his hands and fed the hungry multitude. He reached out with practical compassion to the poor and welcomed those whom society and religion had excluded. In all this he showed us what God is like. In consequence, he was able to make the astounding claim, 'Whoever has seen me has seen the Father' (John 14.9).

We can never match the uniqueness or the perfection of Jesus, but we can learn from his example by daily offering to God the work of our hands. For instance, it is recorded of Jesus, 'In the morning, while it was still very dark, he got up and went out to a deserted place, and there he prayed' (Mark 1.35). I am not suggesting for one moment that we should all follow his example of getting up to pray before the crack of dawn. Such a practice might suit the personality type or biological make-up of some, but by no means all. It would leave most of us shattered for the rest of the day! Nor do I want to induce guilt in busy people by drawing the inference that despite the busyness of our Lord's life, he found time to pray. No! It goes deeper and is more important than that. I believe that his busyness was so wonderfully purposeful and effective because he offered it to God each day. It is an example we can follow in a manner that is true to our personality and temperament, as well as meaningful within our particular circumstances.

A parental care

We can also learn from our Lord's unshakable confidence that God can be trusted to make the best use of what we offer to him. We mustn't be like fussy, inexperienced gardeners, who are forever examining the progress of their plants and 'hurrying them along'. We mustn't waste time constantly taking our spiritual temperature, measuring our progress by the volume of our Christian work, the success rate of our prayers, or, God forbid, the number of Christian committees we are on! Having offered the work of our hands to God, we must allow him to work through us in his own way and in his own time. We must resist the temptation to be God-botherers.

Jesus had to get to grips with this kind of issue early in his public ministry. That is what the temptations in the wilderness were all about. Whatever material, spiritual or psychological interpretation we may place upon them, they were designed to make Jesus force the hand of God: surely his Father would not stand by and watch his Son perish through lack of food, or fail to intervene miraculously as he plunged earthward from the pinnacle of the Temple? (Matthew 4.1–11). Jesus was being tempted to make a kind of pre-emptive strike and gain popularity and power.

But he would have none of it. He had placed the work of his hands in the hands of God and was content to leave it there. He would not force God's hand by behaving selfishly and foolishly. He would trust in the faithfulness of his Father in heaven. What was true of his life and work was also true of his death. This trust in his Father, though sorely tried as he suffered the ignominious agony and death of the cross, held firm to the end. His final words from the cross were, 'Father, into your hands I commend my spirit' (Luke 23.46).

The parental 'hands of God' are the safest place in all the world to be, for they are motherly-fatherly hands of compassion and care, a truth taught in one of the most beautiful biblical insights from the Old Testament (Isaiah 49.15–16) where, because of their experience of being in captivity, the people of God were convinced that he had forgotten them. He corrected their mistaken impression by describing in graphic terms the motherly-fatherly nature of his care for them.

> Can a woman forget her nursing-child,
>   or show no compassion for the
>   child of her womb?
> Even these may forget,
>   yet I will not forget you.

> See, I have inscribed you on the palms
> of my hands;
> your walls are continually
> before me.

I can never read these verses from Isaiah without recalling the practice of many young people of writing in ink on the palms of their hands, names and numbers they wish to remember. It may seem a strange practice, but probably more effective than tying a knot in a handkerchief, as some adults do. Using their hands so much during the course of the day, they are constantly reminded of what they wish to remember. So it is with God our Father. Even when others forget, he remembers.

Of course God has no physical hands like us but, in describing the mystery and majesty of God's character and care, we are forced to use human language despite its obvious limitations. Nevertheless, the picture presented in Isaiah of God inscribing our names on the palms of his hands provides an image of great comfort and encouragement. When God, to use human language, lifts his hands to perform his work of creativity and care, our names are always before him. He cannot and will not forget us.

It is with confidence, therefore, that we can place ourselves and the work of our hands into the hands of God each day.

2
Eyes

I have always been a fan of P. G. Wodehouse. His characters are memorable, his turn of phrase unforgettable. And none more so than when he described a character in one of his novels as having 'the sort of eye that can open an oyster at sixty paces'. It was his inimitable way of saying that eyes can be very powerful organs. He was absolutely right. Not only can they receive and register information; they can also inform and influence. They can send messages of love or hate, tenderness or cruelty, welcome or warning.

It is a fact confirmed by personal experience. Most of us have been on the receiving end of such messages. We can tell when words of welcome are accompanied by a smile that reaches the eyes. And we know when a preoccupied, distracted look contradicts the welcoming words being spoken. We've all suffered the humiliation of talking to those who are marvellously skilled at smiling and nodding superficially, while their eyes are searching the room for someone more important to talk to. Conversely, we have been affirmed and encouraged when someone has focused a look of interest and attention upon us and valued who we are and what we had to say.

Eyes are rarely neutral. They are always saying something. They act as mirrors, registering what we see in others; and they serve as windows, revealing those things we might prefer to hide from others. Disconcerting though it may be, some believe that our eyes are the organs through which our intelligence, or lack of it, is revealed. How important it is, therefore, to offer the use of our eyes, and all that they symbolize, to God each day, and to invite him to be in our eyes and in our looking, that we may see as he sees. For things are not always as they seem to be.

Appearances can deceive

What we see is not always what we get. Those charged with choosing people for responsible positions in society or in the church know this only too well. The curriculum vitae of a candidate may make him or her an obvious choice for shortlisting; indeed, on paper they seem to have all the qualifications of the archangel Gabriel. Yet, five minutes into their subsequent interview, it becomes blindingly clear that they would be like a square peg in a round hole. How they looked on paper was at variance with how they appeared and performed in reality. Occasionally, the same thing happens in reverse. Someone who crept on to the shortlist because others dropped out is revealed as a star, so outstanding as to make his or her appointment inevitable.

Samuel, the prophet charged with the responsibility of finding and anointing a successor to Saul as king of Israel, had a similar experience (1 Samuel 16.1–13). Told by God that his shortlist was exclusively made up of the sons of Jesse, he went to Bethlehem to interview them. Seven of Jesse's sons were paraded before Samuel and, as far as he was concerned, they were 'the magnificent seven'. All were impressive and he was convinced that among them must be God's chosen one. But he was wrong. God gave all seven the thumbs down.

Samuel, it seems, was applying a false criterion and coming up with the wrong result. He was basing his judgement and selection procedure on outward appearance, and thought he saw the future king among the seven. God didn't look at outward appearance but on the heart – and rejected the lot of them. Finally Samuel, discovering that Jesse's youngest son, David, had been excluded by his father from the shortlist, asked for him to be brought from minding the sheep to be interviewed. As soon as he appeared before Samuel, God said, 'Rise and anoint him; for this is the one' (1 Samuel 16.12).

The oak in the acorn

The method of choosing David in preference to his brothers would certainly not have satisfied today's equal opportunities legislation but, despite some human failures on the way, he became an outstanding king. God sees people and things as they really are. We will never have the all-knowing ability of God. Like David, we will encounter human frailties and failures along the way. But if we offer our eyes to God and ask that we may more and more begin to see things and people as he sees them, it will transform our approach to so many aspects of life.

John is a perfect example of what I mean, as I discovered recently while doing some work in the inner city. I had been invited to spend a week in the area, living and working with the people, getting to know their problems and assessing their opportunities. I was there to help but, as so often happens, received help and inspiration myself – and much of it came from the example of John and his impact upon his locality. He maintained a low personal profile, but within his local community his influence, though hidden, was deeply significant. The highlight of my week was the unsolicited community-wide testimony to his creative, visionary activity. 'He always sees the oak in the acorn,' was the way people described him. In a socially deprived area, where leadership skills were severely limited, John had the vision and the ability to spot potential leaders and to help them fulfil their potential.

He not only valued people as they were but also had the vision to see what they would become. He saw people, as it were, through the eyes of Jesus and, like him, discerned the oak in the acorn. That was the hallmark of the ministry of Jesus. He didn't ask for volunteers to join his early band of disciples. He chose people and called them to follow. His choice fell on a most unlikely and insignificant group of people. But he saw what they would become, and was prepared to work patiently with them as the prospective leaders of his mission.

Among that group was Peter, who became the leader of the

Church in those early days. At first glance he wasn't exactly executive material – a bluff, loud, extrovert and unpredictable fisherman, capable of total devotion and abject denial. Life with Peter promised to be a roller-coaster experience, for stability was not one of his early characteristics. But Jesus saw in him the one who ultimately would bring rocklike qualities of leadership to his Church (Matthew 16.13–20).

And who would have considered a religious bigot like Saul of Tarsus to be promising material for leadership in the Church, which he had persecuted and tried to destroy? Yet Jesus saw in Saul, to be renamed Paul, the one person with the ideal qualities to lead his mission to the gentile world. He confronted him in a life-transforming encounter on the Damascus road and, by the grace of God, Paul became the most powerful human personality in the history of the Church (Acts 9.1–9).

The ability to see the potential in others and to nurture it towards realization is a gift from God. It is a source of enrichment not only to the person concerned but also to the community in which they live. We all need to pause from time to time and, looking back over our lives, give thanks to God for those who unselfishly, patiently and creatively nurtured the potential they first saw in us. At the same time, we may need to ask God to help us to see through his eyes in order that, within the network of our relationships, we may discern the potential in others and encourage its fulfilment.

Eyes of compassion

But if we invite God to help us in our looking, it may open up all kinds of new challenges and opportunities that will demand our practical response.

That was certainly true of Jesus. When confronted with a great crowd of hungry people, his disciples panicked, and asked him to send them away, because they presented an insoluble administrative problem. Jesus refused to do so. He saw the people not as a problem but as sheep without a shepherd and offered them practical compassion – he fed them! (Mark 6.30–44). On another occasion, as Jesus was moving with his disciples towards Jerusalem, some of them were intent on getting the best seats in what they imagined would be the administration of his earthly kingdom (Matthew 20.20–28). But as Jesus stood over Jerusalem seats were the last thing on his mind. His eyes were filled with tears. His compassion was stirred because he saw the tragedy of a city, and its religious system that was blind to its real need, dismissive of God's offer of peace and renewal, and pursuing priorities that would bring destruction upon itself (Luke 19.41–44). He saw impending disaster and wept tears of compassion.

That same compassion was also shown to those whom others despised, excluded or victimized as of little value to society. He saw, understood and affirmed their true worth and offered them practical help, feeding their hunger, healing their sickness, and breaking down the religious barriers that excluded them.

As it was with Jesus, so it will be with us. If we look through eyes of compassion, we shall see, we shall understand, and we shall respond in practical terms. As in the case of Jane, that may result in a major upheaval in our way of life. She saw the interview with the six-year-old Afghan refugee who, when asked, 'What would you like more than anything else in the world?', replied, 'Bread'. It marked the beginning of a compassionate understanding that eventually led to a secondment from her teaching post to work for two years with an aid agency in Afghanistan.

For Sarah and Paul, it was different. They didn't leave home, they simply opened the doors of their house even wider. A fairly ordinary couple, they had nurtured their own three children wisely and well. But they saw and understood the plight of children who, through no fault of their own, were being deprived of love and care. Their response was to open their home to numerous foster-children, and to work wonders with some difficult and disturbed teenagers. With compassion, sensitivity and skill, they have created a home where strangers are welcome and valued.

Others respond to need in less dramatic, though equally committed, ways. Sam, himself a pensioner, cuts the grass and tends the gardens of three rather frail widows. Annette, a retired head teacher, provides a voluntary taxi service for elderly patients needing to attend appointments at the local hospital. Margaret, a gentle and cheerful spinster, goes one day every week to a friend suffering from dementia, and sits with her while her husband has the periodic break that is so vital for his health and sanity.

All of these, and scores of others like them, are the eyes and hands of God through which his compassion is given practical expression. They not only find shape and purpose for their own lives and bring help to those they serve, but they also provide a vital caring ingredient within the life of their community. And it is within the life of the community, wherever that community may be, that we must expect to have that most important of all experiences, namely, seeing God.

Seeing God in others

It was Anselm, the eleventh-century Archbishop of Canterbury, who said, 'I was created to see God, and I have not yet accomplished that for which I was made' (Ward and Wild, 1997). He was right on both counts. Christians believe that to see God face to face is the crowning experience and culmination of their journey of faith. However, the fullness of that experience and vision will not be realized in this life but in the next. For the moment, as St Paul reminds us, 'We see through a mirror, dimly, but then, face to face' (1 Corinthians 13.12). For the moment, we live each day by faith and not by sight, but always in the sure expectation that, ultimately, 'We will be like him, for we will see him as he is' (1 John 3.2). We shall accomplish that for which we were created!

Nevertheless, though the unclouded vision of God is, for the moment, beyond us, we can see glimpses of God in the world and in other people. Through our knowledge of the scriptures and the ministry of the Holy Spirit, we see him revealed in a unique way in Jesus Christ, so that God is no stranger to us. But we must also expect to see him in other people.

That should not surprise us. John wrote, 'All things came into being through him, and without him not one thing came into being. What has come into being in him was life, and the life was the light of all people' (John 1.3–4). We should expect, therefore, to catch glimpses of God in his creation, and especially in those who have been made in his image. As we noted earlier, it was out of such conviction that George Herbert was able to write in his wonderful hymn, 'Teach me my God and King, in all things thee to see.'

We need to begin each new day with a similar prayer and conviction. We need to move into the day with the hopeful expectation that, with our eyes and minds offered to God and focused by faith, we may see him in the lives of other people. It was Jesus himself who taught us to look with such purpose and expectation when he told the parable of the judgement (Matthew 25.31–46). It has some surprising and rather uncomfortable insights. When people perform good deeds for other poorer human beings, they are in fact ministering to Jesus himself. We can discover Jesus in a lonely neighbour, a refugee, a troubled teenager, a single parent, or someone dying and in need of comfort. As we identify with the pain of others, we show the face of God to them, and sometimes, in their vulnerability and need, we see the face of God.

Lawrence Freeman, an English Benedictine, wrote, 'To see God is not to see anything extraordinary but to see ordinary things as they really are' (Ward and Wild, 1997). Giving bread to hungry children in Afghanistan, opening our homes or using our resources to help needy people, or sitting quietly and with compassion alongside someone with dementia may all seem fairly ordinary. But if we have eyes to see these ordinary things as they really are, we may catch a glimpse of the glory and footprints of God, and follow in his steps.

3
Mouth

Those who have ever been to Southwell Minster will understand why I love the place. Dominating the small country town of Southwell, near Newark, it has a majestic, yet simple charm and is one of the most beautiful Norman buildings in Europe. It contains many architectural gems, including the famous 'Leaves of Southwell' – an outstanding display of foliage carved in stone and adorning the Chapter House. But my favourite carving is not the 'Leaves', but one of the many heads that have been carved around the crown of some of the small pillars. The 'Leaves' always cause me to sigh with wonder and delight at their intricate beauty. My favourite 'head', however, never fails to bring a smile to my lips and a sense of fun to my heart. It portrays a woman with a gag over her mouth!

As you can imagine, all kinds of explanations are given as to the significance of it, including a few politically incorrect ones, but I treat most of them with some scepticism. Far from portraying a talkative person, who was forced, as it were, to 'put a sock in it', I much prefer to see it as representing a wise woman who knew her Bible well and took appropriate action. Indeed, she might well have taken to heart some words from the psalmist when he prayed, 'Set a guard over my mouth, O LORD; keep watch over the door of my lips' (Psalm 141.3), or decided to follow his example when he said, 'I will keep a muzzle on my mouth' (Psalm 39.1).

We may never know what was in the mind of the stonemason when he carved the head of the woman with the gag over her mouth. He, or his employer, may have had a tongue-lashing from an angry wife – and might well have deserved it. The woman concerned could be demonstrating the only proper response to belligerence, namely silence. She might even have been suffering from toothache. But the one thing we do know is that words are a powerful force for good and evil. Much thought must be given and great care taken before speaking them – a message that my favourite head delivers with humour and pertinence.

Tongues on fire

It was James, in his New Testament letter, who delivered the most devastating description of the power of words. He likened the tongue to a fire, a spark from which could set a whole forest ablaze (James 3.1–10). He was not wrong. And most of us will have witnessed the power of words to destroy. All too often we have seen it happen in the political arena when careless words have been spoken, perhaps in a religious, racial or sectarian context, and destructive controversy and conflict has followed.

But we also see it in personal life, where words, carelessly or maliciously used, can destroy the character of others and bring about bitterness within families and communities. My pastoral ministry over many years has taken me into some most contentious family situations, where words spoken in the past have caused deep hurt and never been forgotten nor forgiven. And this hurt tends to surface on those occasions, like weddings and funerals, when emotions are running fairly high. There have been times when I have felt more like a referee than a priest.

The same is true of communities. When I was Bishop of Bradford, the words written by Salman Rushdie in his book *Satanic Verses* resulted in book burning and community unrest. Some found his words inspiring. Others considered them insulting and an attack upon their identity as Muslims. It was indeed a spark that lit a very large fire, the heat from which was felt across the world.

For most of us, however, the experience of tongues of fire is more limited, but at times no less devastating – though the person with the inflammatory tongue is often blissfully unaware of the damage being caused. Duncan was a classic example. He thought he was God's gift to the church but in reality was a walking disaster area. It wasn't that his words were vitriolic, but they were voluble – non-stop. He hadn't simply kissed the blarney stone; he had swallowed it, refusing to use one word if twenty would do.

Duncan wasn't just an incessant talker. He was a dedicated gossip, a kind of human e-mail. Information gleaned from his conversation with one person was speedily spread across the local community – and it never lost anything in the telling! To begin with, people laughed at Duncan and his uncontrolled tongue. But their laughter turned to anxiety and then to anger, when they realized that confidences were being shared and wrong impressions created. Information being relayed back to the people concerned bore no resemblance to reality. Fellowship within the church and the wider community was suffering, so he had to be taken to one side and, with the help of the epistle of James, gently but firmly admonished regarding the misuse of his tongue. Thankfully, he eventually got the message and changed his ways, but it was painful. Fences had to be mended and bridges rebuilt before trust was re-established.

Fortunately, people like Duncan are the exception. There are many more people whose words, far from creating havoc, produce harmony and bring healing instead of hurt. Elizabeth was such a person. She had a way with words but used them sparingly. People found her easy to talk to and many of them shared their personal problems with her. They knew she would be utterly discreet, and her response was always thoughtful and wise. Time and again when a reconciling presence was needed, Elizabeth's help was sought, and she frequently brought order out of confusion. People trusted her. She enhanced the life of every group to which she belonged, building confidence between people rather than creating chaos.

A God who speaks

It is in bringing order out of chaos that God is first presented as one who speaks. He called creation into being. He said, 'Let there be light'; and there was light. He spoke, and creation developed from form to fullness as birds filled the skies, fish filled the seas and human creatures began to occupy the earth (Genesis 1–2). And over the centuries to the present day, God has spoken. He has spoken not only in creation, but also in history, through the prophets, through the scriptures and, supremely, he has spoken in his Son, Jesus Christ. This is a truth that holds great possibilities for the use of our mouths and the words we speak. The recognition of the power of words for good and evil, together with the recollection that the God we worship is one who speaks, provides us with the incentive to ask God to be in our mouths and in our speaking.

That God should be in our mouths and in our speaking is not a pious image without substance. It has a very practical application to daily life, for words are the things we use most each day. They are vital for communication and the building of relationships. This glorious faculty, therefore, must not be taken for granted, but humbly offered to God each day so that the words we speak, far from being wasted, become a powerful influence for good.

I am not suggesting that God should fill our conversation with Bible texts or that we should be like a ventriloquist's dummy, with God twiddling the knobs and putting words in our mouth. Nor am I talking about a holy language made up of so-called Christian words. On the contrary, I am talking about the kind of speaking that resonates with the reality of the circumstances surrounding the one who is listening, and that brings a distinctive quality to every act of communication, wherever and with whomsoever it takes place.

'People talking without speaking' is a line from 'Sound of Silence', the song sung by Simon and Garfunkel, and it has always impressed me by its perceptiveness – for it is painfully true. Talking is not necessarily the same as speaking. Haven't we all suffered from those who can talk for hours and say nothing? And haven't we all benefited from those who say little but speak to the heart? We know and can recognize the voice that speaks to us in the depth of our being.

The Greeks had a delicate way of indicating that speech is not improved by wordiness. Their expression for silence was 'good speech'. They had a point. And certainly in the scriptures, the silences of God are as profound as his words. For God as well as for us, there is a time to speak and a time to keep silent. When God spoke and renewed his call to the prophet Elijah at the mouth of the cave at Horeb, he did so not in the spectacular extravaganza of wind, earthquake and fire, but in 'a sound of sheer silence' (1 Kings 19.11–18). It was a word that penetrated his heart.

Messengers of God

Elijah found, like many others, that God speaks in a variety of ways and through a variety of people. And one of the reasons why it is of practical importance to ask that God may be in our mouths and in our speaking is that he is able and willing to speak through ordinary people like you and me. And many of us will have experience of life-changing conversations, when the words of a friend, and sometimes of an enemy, have become a word from God to us. They have come like a hammer blow to bring us to our senses, or shone like a beacon to show us the way ahead.

Jonathan was a beacon who shone at the right time! It was Easter Sunday morning and I was indoors recovering slowly from a serious heart attack. My family had gone to the local parish church for the Easter celebration, and I sat alone in the small chapel at the bishop's house in Bradford. To be honest, though it was Easter, I didn't feel like celebrating. In fact, I was downright miserable and full of self-pity. What had I done to deserve this? A bishop should be in his cathedral on Easter Sunday morning, leading the faithful in worship, but here was I, alone, crushed with a sense of failure, and not particularly pleased with God.

The doorbell rang. I almost didn't answer it but will be forever thankful that I did. It was Jonathan. I recognized him as an eleven-year-old boy I had confirmed just before my heart attack. In his hand he held a small, but rather beautiful, candle. He smiled and said, 'Bishop Roy, this is a candle from off the altar of my parish church. It comes with the love and prayers of the congregation. It comes to assure you that you are not forgotten.' It was a defining moment for me. Jonathan had not just brought a message; he was the message. His words came like a hammer blow to my feelings of self-pity, and they shone like a beacon on the way ahead. He was a visible and tangible word from God, renewing my life and vision.

It is a thrilling thought that God may use our mouths to speak words that will influence other people. But it can also be a rather terrifying prospect and, perhaps, one of the reasons why God gave us two ears and only one mouth. We need to listen much and speak little. We need to listen carefully and hear perceptively before we can speak effectively to other people.

We must remember that most people are just like us. They may have personal problems that cause them anxiety, family concerns that worry them, past events that still haunt them, or uncertainties about the future that cause them to lie awake at night. They don't assume that we, their friends and acquaintances, are gurus or guiding lights. They neither expect nor require us always to be the voice of God to them – what arrogant bores we would become if we ever thought of ourselves as such! We are not sent to them as prophets, we come to them as friends, who need to be relaxed and natural in their presence, and not constantly looking for the opportunity to speak a profound and definitive word to them.

Yet we know that words, innocently spoken, can produce pleasure or pain, joy or sorrow. They can heal and they can hurt. They can bring comfort and they can bring distress. And if we thought too much about it, we wouldn't talk to anyone lest we upset them. But we know there is a better way, a way that could help us to enrich every conversation in which we share, whatever the topic, be it shopping or salvation, holidays or heaven. It is to follow the example of the psalmist and say, 'Set a guard over my mouth, O LORD; keep watch over the door of my lips' (Psalm 141.3). Far from imposing frustrating restrictions on our words, such guardianship of our mouths would enable more of our talking to become speaking.

A voice from within

According to the scriptures, talking and speaking come from within, and reveal the kind of person we really are. That is the clear teaching of Jesus and caused him to utter the most fearsome warning about the words we speak. 'I tell you, on the day of judgement you will have to give an account for every careless word you utter; for by your words you will be justified, and by your words you will be condemned' (Matthew 12.36–37). These are strong words that need to be put in context.

Jesus was speaking to the Pharisees. They had become so blind in their prejudice against him that they couldn't recognize goodness when they saw it! They rejected his teaching, and declared that the power by which he healed people came not from God but from the devil. But in calling good evil, they were revealing the distortion and darkness within themselves. Their careless, irresponsible and malicious words about Jesus spoke volumes about the state of their own hearts – 'For out of the abundance of the heart the mouth speaks' (Matthew 12.34) – a point that Jesus pressed home by using the metaphor of the tree and its fruit. As the nature of the tree is judged by the fruit it produces, so the true nature of a person is to be judged by the words they speak.

All this helps us to understand what Jesus meant in his strong warning about being held to account for the words we speak. He was not implying that God had the use of a personal computer, and one day would process every word we had ever spoken and hold us to account. We mustn't reduce God to a kind of ecclesiastical watchdog. He is not a God of trivia and revenge but of truth and love. His warning was directed at 'careless' words, that is, words spoken irresponsibly and without thought, that distort the truth about other people and about ourselves. Such words give a false impression of others, undermining their character and misrepresenting their point of view and, perhaps, presenting ourselves as paragons of virtue at their expense. That is certainly what the Pharisees were doing and why Jesus spoke so firmly to them.

None of us is immune from the possibility of uttering careless words for which we shall be held to account. So once again, we see the practical wisdom of the psalmist in asking God to put a guard on his mouth and to keep a watch over his lips. Remarkably, the psalmist was offering a prayer to God at the time. He wasn't just thinking of what he might say to others; he was also concerned about what he said to God and, perhaps, how he might say it.

Job had a similar concern when, towards the end of his dispute with God regarding the truth behind the sufferings he was enduring, he said, 'I will lay my hand on my mouth' (Job 40.4). In other words he would be quiet and let God speak. And God did so, with great effect, so that at the end of his dramatic words, Job replied, 'I have uttered what I did not understand... but now my eyes see you, therefore I despise myself and repent in dust and ashes' (Job 42.3–6).

It is a lesson we all need to take to heart. Even when we come into the presence of God to pray, perhaps we should begin by placing our hand over our mouth. By doing so, we would acknowledge our need to listen before we speak. It would also be a recognition of our ignorance in comparison to his limitless knowledge and wisdom.

Perhaps my favourite 'head' in Southwell Minster, as well as bringing a smile to our lips, might also convey a message to our tongues. In our conversing with God and other people, there is a time to speak and a time to be silent.

4
Heart

John Wesley, one of the greatest and most influential preachers in the history of the Church, described the moment of his conversion in these terms, 'I felt my heart strangely warmed... I felt I did trust in Christ.' Wesley, an Oxford scholar and Anglican priest, had made a trip to Georgia to convert the Americans, but learned from the experience that he was the one needing to be converted. The influence of domineering parents had ensured that his was a religion of orthodoxy and morality rather than love and joy. All that changed when, on 24 May 1738, he attended a Meeting House in Aldersgate Street, London. It was there, while listening to a missionary expounding Martin Luther's commentary on St Paul's letter to the Romans, that his troubled heart was 'strangely warmed' and, as it were, he broke through the faith barrier. It marked a dramatic change in his life and in the nature and direction of his ministry.

But, though dramatic and life-changing, Wesley's experience is not unique. Certainly the description of his heart being strangely warmed is both beautiful and peculiarly his, but a spiritual conversion that reaches the heart is an experience that has been enjoyed by countless people throughout the ages. For some it happens in exciting or emotional ways; for others it emerges as a quiet awareness of a presence within, or the culmination of a gradual process. But for all, sooner or later, it touches the heart and for most determines the shape and priorities of life.

The hidden centre

That such an experience should be life – transforming is not surprising. For in the scriptures the heart refers to the inward centre of the person, not to mere feelings and emotions but to the whole person in relation to God. The heart is the focus of our inner personal life, the source of motives, passion, thought and conscience, the seat of our collective energies. That which touches and embraces the heart, whether it be the love of God, the love of material things, or the pursuit of selfish ambition, will inevitably shape the way we live. That was the point Jesus made when he said, 'Where your treasure is, there your heart will be also' (Matthew 6.21).

This particular truth was demonstrated by two of my teenage friends. They had each been born with a silver spoon in their mouths. John's parents owned a flourishing garage. Mary's parents were doctors who themselves had inherited considerable wealth. Both Mary and John were delightful characters. They had open, unspoilt, generous and loyal personalities that remained unchanged when, on the death of their parents, each came into a substantial inheritance.

To this day they retain their attractive, outgoing personalities, but their hearts have taken them in different directions. John is the managing director of a very successful business. Everything he touches turns to gold, and his commercial interests now spread far and wide. The demands upon him are heavy, and his time and energies are consumed making contacts and doing deals. In a competitive age, that is neither surprising nor a cause for carping criticism. But though he remains friendly, open and generous, he is, by his own admission, committed to making money. He is very scathing about religion and fairly sceptical about God, though recently, when someone referred rather dismissively to the direction Mary's life had taken, he replied sharply, 'Don't knock it.'

The pathway Mary has chosen is certainly different. She obtained an honours degree in English and for a while taught in a local secondary school. Following her marriage to Eric, and the arrival of the first of her three children, she retired from the teaching profession, and gave herself to the care of her family and a continuous supply of foster children. With sensitivity and skill, Mary and Eric have worked wonders with difficult and disturbed young teenagers and created a home within the community where strangers are welcomed and valued. On top of this, Mary has been Brown Owl of a flourishing Brownie Pack, building up creative links with parents and children throughout the district. She never hides the fact that she is comfortably off, but the treasure that really motivates her are the children in her care.

If asked why her life took the direction it did, Mary is forthright in saying, with humble assurance, 'It is God's doing.' During a university mission, she had become aware of the incredible generosity of God's love in sending his Son to die in order that she might have life. In response, to use her own words, 'It seemed right that I should give my heart to him.' That experience, and the manner in which she described it, might not resonate with everyone, though it undoubtedly does with me and finds an echo in my own experience. It certainly proved to be life-transforming for Mary.

It would be unfair and unwise to draw the automatic conclusion, 'big business bad, family life good'. That is not the point. In living their full and purposeful lives, John and Mary each followed their heart. In each case, the motivating force was strong but different. Personal ambition and love of material success appeared to reign supreme in John's heart and was clearly the driving force of his life. As for Mary, the love of God seemed to fill her home and her heart, causing her to reach out in love to other people, especially children.

In both cases, life was shaped by the desire and, some would say, the vision of the heart.

Seeing rightly

The vision of the heart may seem a strange notion but there is real substance to it. The French novelist Antoine de Saint-Exupéry, in his children's book *The Little Prince*, wrote this: 'It is only with the heart that one can see rightly; what is essential is invisible to the eye.' He is not alone in his conviction that it is only with the heart that we can see things as they really are.

Heart

St Paul felt the same way and says so in his letter to the Ephesians (1.15–23). In this quite remarkable passage of scripture, we overhear Paul praying that the Holy Spirit will be at work in the lives of his readers. The breadth of his vision of God is matched by the depth of his prayers for them. He asks that they may have a practical understanding of what God has done for them in Christ. He desires that they may be aware of God's plan for history and the world, and how they are to live in the light of it. He not only tells them how they are to know these things, but prays for it to happen, 'so that, with the eyes of your heart enlightened, you may know what is the hope to which he has called you' (Ephesians 1.18).

We can all remember times when the eyes of our heart were more perceptive than those in our head, times when we were able to see, as it were, behind the veneer of some person or problem and make a decision that seemed dubious then but later proved to be right.

I vividly recall a mother and father coming to see me with their six children, the youngest of whom was a babe in arms, and the reason for their visit. They wanted her baptized because the vicar where they lived had refused to do it. Apparently, having baptized the other five without any sign that they were interested in coming to church, he had refused number six – and who can blame him? I certainly didn't, and told the couple so, but I had what I can only describe as a 'niggle' deep down in my heart.

The father told me that the family were moving into my parish because they had outgrown their present house. He looked both ill and anxious and, on reflection, it was this fact that touched and enlightened the eyes of my heart and caused me to see rightly. As we talked together over a period of weeks, it became clear that his illness was terminal. Having only a few months to live, he wanted to see his wife and family settled in their new home and his youngest child 'done' properly!

Having given some basic Christian teaching to both parents, I baptized their child with pleasure and welcomed the whole family into the church. With the help of an understanding and compassionate congregation, they became regular worshippers and were supported fully when the father died some months later.

To be fair, not all decisions of the heart turn out so well, and I have pangs of conscience and remorse when I recall those occasions when I have let my heart rule my head and lived to regret it. A willingness, for instance, to have faith in someone who has fallen and in need of help has sometimes resulted in a betrayal of trust, and hurt being afflicted on other people. And there have also been occasions when my hardness of heart, usually caused by frustration at not getting my own way, has made me stubborn and unyielding. My prejudices have masqueraded as principles and the work of God has suffered.

It is all part of life, of course, but it emphasizes the need not to take our hearts for granted but to recognize the need for constant vigilance. For out of the same mouth and, therefore, the same heart come blessing and cursing (James 3.10).

A heart divided

It is this potential inconsistency that made the psalmist ask God to give him an undivided heart, that is, a heart united in purpose and devoted to God (Psalm 86.11). It was a prayer offered out of the murky depths of his experience! In choosing David to be king of Israel, God had assessed him as 'a man after his own heart' (1 Samuel 13.14). He became a great king and did wonderful things for God and his people, but his heart was not always united. Indeed at times it was painfully, even sinfully, divided, a fact that became tragically evident when he let God and himself down by bringing injustice and hurt upon the household of Bathsheba (2 Samuel 11–12).

Recognizing his moral failure and folly, David described his remorse and repentance in one of his penitential psalms:

> Have mercy on me, O God,
>   according to your steadfast love;
> according to your abundant mercy
>   blot out my transgressions.

> Wash me thoroughly from my
> iniquity,
> and cleanse me from my sin.
> (Psalm 51.1–2)

It is a salutary reminder that no matter how mature we may consider ourselves to be as followers of Christ, our hearts are not immune to the pressures and temptations of life and the subtleties of sin. There are times when our heart can deceive us.

One of the first Bible verses I was taught as a new Christian came as a bit of a shock. 'The heart is devious above all else; it is perverse – who can understand it?' (Jeremiah 17.9). Of course, such a stark description of the human heart had a specific application to Jeremiah's situation, but it cannot be dismissed as an anachronism. David, from bitter experience, wouldn't have done so. Nor would Paul, who spoke graphically of his own inner conflict: 'For I do not do the good I want, but the evil I do not want is what I do' (Romans 7.19). Nor, indeed, would most of us if we are prepared to be honest with ourselves and with God.

We have all suffered from a divided heart on those occasions when, despite our desire to be loyal and do the right thing, our thoughts, words or deeds have shamed us and dishonoured God. There are times when our motives are so mixed that we are not sure if we are doing God's will or our own. On other occasions, we get things so out of perspective that we even try to pull the wool over God's eyes. How often, for instance, have we prayed in such a manner as to claim God for our side over against those who oppose or disagree with us, when in reality he is fed up with both of us for behaving like spoilt children! In the light of such things there is no room for complacency but every need for vigilance and care.

Because of my medical history, my doctor regularly tells me, 'Take care of your heart.' It is not only sound medical advice but also excellent spiritual counsel, fully supported by the wisdom of God: 'Keep your heart with all vigilance, for from it flow the springs of life' (Proverbs 4.23).

Given that the heart is the centre of our whole person in relation to God, we certainly need to watch over it, to ensure that the springs of life which flow from it are unified and pure rather than devious and divided. Thankfully, we are not left to do this in our own strength. There is help available.

A heart renewed

It was King David, full of remorse and repentance for his moral failure in connection with Bathsheba, who cried out for the help of God in transforming his divided, sinful heart:

> Create in me a clean heart, O God,
>   and put a new and right spirit
>   within me.
> Do not cast me away from your
>   presence,
>   and do not take your holy spirit
>   from me.
> Restore to me the joy of your
>   salvation,
>   and sustain in me a willing spirit.
>   (Psalm 51.10–12)

By using the word 'create', David was asking for a miracle; nothing less will do. God alone can provide a clean heart and a new spirit. David wanted a radical renewal that would restore the springs of life, the sense of forgiveness, joy, consistency and loyalty that he knew when he first became king.

It was the same deep-seated longing, which the people of God have expressed in every age and to which he has responded with such reassurance and generosity. We see it first when God promised a renewal of heart to his people when they returned from exile:

> A new heart I will give you, and a new spirit I will put within you; and I will remove from your body the heart of

stone and give you a heart of flesh. I will put my spirit within you, and make you follow my statutes and be careful to observe my ordinances.

(Ezekiel 36.26–27)

To those broken in heart and spirit by the devastating experience of being carried into captivity, God promises that he will replace their heart of stone with a heart of flesh. The stubborn, rebellious and insensitive heart that had led to their exile in a foreign land will be replaced with a soft, impressionable and responsive heart. And the spirit of disobedience that they carried with them into captivity will be replaced by his spirit, that will transform and empower them to follow God's right way of living. This way of living was not merely inscribed upon tablets of stone, like the Ten Commandments given to Moses, and disregarded in disobedience, but imprinted, by his spirit, upon their hearts, creating a responsiveness to the will of God at the deepest level of their being. It is heart speaking to heart, the God above speaking to the God within us.

It was the renewal that was to find its focus and fulfilment in the person and work of Jesus Christ. Every thing he touched was restored and renewed, whether it was the eyes of the blind, the tongue of the dumb, the limbs of the crippled or the decaying skin of the leper. But, as Paul tells us, he did much more. Through his birth, death and resurrection a new world was born and a new age begun, an age in which all who are in Christ become a new creation, renewed in heart and mind (2 Corinthians 5.16–21).

It is not without significance that John Wesley's 'strangely warmed heart' came at the same moment as he expressed his trust in the person and work of Jesus Christ: 'I felt that I did trust Christ.' His subsequent life and ministry had all the marks of the renewal brought about by his conversion. He understood clearly the teaching of Scripture, that God not only creates a new heart within us, but also requires us to live a renewed life within all the ordinary, awkward, contradictory and frustrating elements of daily life. That, I believe, was what Jesus was doing as he expounded the Sermon on the Mount (Matthew 5–7), which is really a manifesto of God's right way of living. He was revealing a renewed way of being children of God.

Such a challenge cannot be met out of our human resources alone. As part of our daily worship we must offer our heart to God, that out of it may flow those springs of life that will renew us and refresh all those associated with us. We could do no better, perhaps, than accept the advice, and use the words, attributed to Irenaeus (130–202), an early saint of the Church:

> Offer thy heart to God
> In a soft and tractable state
> That it may receive the imprint of
> his fingers
> Lest by being hardened
> Thou miss both his workmanship
> And thy life.

5
Mind

As a lay evangelist in south London in the mid-1950s my job was to visit from house to house for approximately thirty hours each week. It could have been boring, but I found it stimulating – mainly due to the unpredictable nature of what lay on the other side of each door. Metaphorically and physically, it kept me on my toes, ready either to respond to human need or to make a quick getaway if my knock upset an angry dog.

Over the years I discovered that doors, even before they were opened, told me quite a bit about those who lived behind them. For instance, I was at first puzzled, and then thrilled, to learn the significance of the small scroll that was attached to the top of the right doorpost of some houses. It indicated that the occupants of the house were of the Jewish faith. The scroll was a *mezuzah*, containing the *shema* – some verses from the Hebrew Scriptures – which summed up the essential creed of Judaism. 'Hear, O Israel: The LORD is our God, the LORD alone. You shall love the LORD your God with all your heart, and with all your soul, and with all your might' (Deuteronomy 6.4–5). Every Jewish child commits this to memory, knowing that love for God must be wholehearted, involving all that we are and all that we have.

Jesus used the same words in teaching the two great commandments that were to form the basis of Christian life and service. The first was love for God, and the second was love for our neighbour (Mark 12.28–34). But, interestingly, he added the word 'mind' to the list of wholehearted love. What was undoubtedly embraced within the *shema* was made specific by this addition, and has implications for us today. It means that no offering of our love, our worship, our work, our leisure, our service to God and others, will be complete if it does not include the offering of our mind.

A mind suspended

Given that God requires and encourages the offering of our whole selves to him, it is disappointing when some refuse to use their mind or quietly forget they have one. The mind has an important place in the formulation of our faith. Too many people leave their mind at the church door, and are content with an emotional diet aimed at the heart rather than a balanced one that takes in the needs of the mind as well.

Surprisingly, Brenda was like that. She held down a demanding job in a service industry, using her fertile mind to solve awkward personnel problems. At work, she revealed herself as a thoughtful, at times acerbic, team leader. At worship, however, she seemed to undergo a personality change. Her critical faculties were put on hold and she resorted to an emotional involvement in worship that bordered on the banal. She appeared addicted to a pseudo holy language, made up of religious slogans, and wholly unrelated to the nitty-gritty of every day life. The robust thoughtfulness she brought to her professional life was absent from her life within the worshipping community of her local church. To use a sporting term, her mind had been shown the red card! Sadly, she seemed less of a whole person at worship than she was at work.

Derek was in a different category. A geographer by profession, he was a mild man, courteous, kind and reasonable – but not in church. He believed that change of any kind was a retrograde step. An unfamiliar tune to a popular hymn, the reading of the Scriptures in a modern language, or an attitude of compassion towards those seeking remarriage in church after divorce, was roundly and vociferously condemned. As for the suggestion that the church building might be rearranged, with the altar placed in a more central position – he almost had apoplexy at the thought.

When Derek was present at church meetings discussions

were not only heated but also bitter. It wasn't that his mind was closed, for he could argue his case with passion and intellectual skill, but it had become one-track. Tradition was good, change was bad. His mind, which could adjust to, and give reasons for, changes in his professional discipline, was shunted on to a single track when he came to church.

It made life a little difficult – or perhaps more interesting – for others, though it said something for the tolerance and understanding of the church that it was able to welcome and affirm people like Brenda and Derek. Nevertheless, I believe that their local church was all the poorer for their failure to use their minds wisely and well within the community of faith that worshipped there. Suspended, single-track or closed minds not only impoverish our worship and distort our relationships but also bring little glory to the God who created them.

A mind enlarged

Yet one of the functions of the mind is to bring glory to God by giving us greater understanding of his ways. Such understanding is vital if we are to live our lives with purpose and a sense of fulfilment. It was the message underlined by the prophet Jeremiah. At the time in question Israel was fascinated by wisdom, power and wealth. In the nation's pursuit of greatness, these things dominated the thinking of its leaders and people. Jeremiah was convinced, however, that true greatness came through discovering God's priorities and making them our own. His words are perceptive and powerful.

> Thus says the LORD: Do not let the wise boast in their wisdom, do not let the mighty boast in their might, do not let the wealthy boast in their wealth; but let those who boast boast in this, that they understand and know me, that I am the LORD; I act with steadfast love, justice, and righteousness in the earth, for in these things I delight, says the LORD.
>
> (Jeremiah 9.23–24)

The mindless pursuit of wisdom, power and wealth, far from being the pathway to greatness, would prove to be a false trail of diminishing returns, leading to judgement. A genuine opening of the mind towards God, however, would result in an understanding of the way in which he wished them to live. Love, justice and righteousness were things in which he took pleasure and longed to see them reproduced in the lives of his people.

It is as true today as it was then; those who open their mind towards God experience an understanding not only of God himself but also of creation and their place within it. For such understanding is more than mere knowledge or intellectual power. It includes elements of spiritual insight and moral judgement. It opens a window into the ways of God, but it also provides a perceptiveness that enables us to be more aware of the world and the people around us.

I saw this kind of understanding personified in one particular community with whom I lived and worked. Sandra would have been described by most people, including herself, as ordinary. She had left school at fourteen and received no further formal education. Married with two children, she worked part-time as a receptionist in the local doctors' surgery and was involved not only in the life of the church but also in a variety of community activities.

Sandra's faith was strong, her humanity was deep and practical and, in the midst of her busy life, prayer occupied a key place. It was a very powerful combination that resulted in her being a person to whom others came in considerable numbers for guidance, reassurance and inspiration. Her mind, in intellectual terms, would not have been highly rated, but it was remarkably understanding. She didn't wear her religion on her sleeve. Her comments to parents about troubled teenagers, and to teenagers about restrictive parents, were as perceptive and helpful as those she made to any who quizzed her about her faith. She understood people and had, it seemed, a natural ability to be on their wavelength, offering a listening ear, a warm heart and a discerning mind.

She laughed when I compared her to Daniel, and couldn't see the relevance of the comparison until I pointed out that prayer and an open mind were two of the key points of his life and hers. Prayer for Daniel consisted not just in the opening of his windows towards Jerusalem, but in the openness of his mind towards God and what he was doing in his world. 'When I, Daniel, had seen the vision, I tried to understand it' (Daniel 8.15).

Daniel tried to understand and so must we. It isn't always easy for, as God has said, 'My thoughts are not your thoughts, nor are your ways my ways... For as the heavens are higher than the earth, so are my ways higher than your ways and my thoughts than your thoughts' (Isaiah 55.8–9). The truth is, we all have a great distance to go in our understanding of God. We are merely pilgrims on the way. But our journey must be made with an open mind, for of one thing we can be sure, a closed mind will leave little room for growth in understanding.

A mind renewed

But if we are to make progress on our journey of understanding, something more than the absence of a closed, suspended or one-track mind will be needed. We will not reach the end of that journey by default, but by disciplined determination to be renewed in mind. That was the conviction of Paul and it formed an important strand in his message to some of the young churches he was nurturing in the faith.

He saw the renewal of the mind as crucial for progress towards maturity in Christ. When writing to the members of the church at Ephesus, for instance, he exhorted them to 'be renewed in the spirit of your minds' (Ephesians 4.23). He wasn't suggesting a one-off experience of renewal, but rather a continuous process of renewal taking place as we focus on the teachings of Christ (Ephesians 4.20–22).

Paul taught new believers out of his own experience. He remembered how he once had possessed a darkened mind. His understanding was so distorted that he was convinced he was zealously serving God in persecuting Jesus. As a result of his dramatic conversion on the Damascus road, when the light of God shone into his darkness of his inner being, he became a new creature, a new creation in Christ (2 Corinthians 5.17). As a consequence of that new creation Paul received, as do all who are in Christ, a new mind, a mind that is capable of choosing good instead of evil, light instead of darkness, the way of God instead of the way of self.

But we are not expected to sit back passively and let it all happen to us. Divine initiative and human responsibility go hand in hand in the scriptures; there is no such thing as Eliza Doolittle theology. There is no 'Oh, wouldn't it be loverly' in the Bible, no wishful thinking. We are told how to do it: 'Be renewed in the spirit of your minds' (Ephesians 4.23). Our mind is to be renewed by exercising our faculties on new subjects. We are to focus on the new lifestyle which our new creation demands, setting aside our old selfish ways of living, and focusing on those new ways of life that will make it clear that God is in control of our lives. Right thinking will result in right living. We are to put off old ways and put on new ways (Ephesians 4.17–32).

Paul taught the same truth in his letter to the Christians at Rome. The worship that God describes as spiritual and acceptable is the offering of our whole selves, including our powers of thought and reason, namely our renewed mind.

> I appeal to you therefore, brothers and sisters, by the mercies of God, to present your bodies as a living sacrifice, holy and acceptable to God, which is your spiritual worship. Do not be conformed to this world, but be transformed by the renewing of your minds, so that you may discern what is the will of God – what is good and acceptable and perfect.
>
> (Romans 12.1–2)

Paul's words are pertinent and persuasive. Christians are to offer their whole selves to God as a response to the mercy he has shown them in Christ, through whose death and resurrection they have been made a new creation. Since they belong to God's new age, which began with the coming of Christ, they must resist the pressures of 'this world, this present age', to mould them according to its own standards and values. Instead, they must open themselves to the influence of the Holy Spirit who will renew their minds, enabling them to discern God's will and equipping them with the power to do it.

Discovering God's will is never easy, for he doesn't reduce it to a set of rules and regulations. It wasn't easy for Paul, and other believers, in the Roman society of his day, nor is it easy for us in our complex and fragmented society. But with our minds renewed by the Spirit of God and focused on the person and work of Christ, it becomes gloriously possible.

The mind of Christ

It becomes gloriously possible because, with the renewing of our minds by the Holy Spirit, we have the mind of Christ. This sounds like a dreadfully arrogant claim but there is clear biblical justification for it. 'We have the mind of Christ', said Paul when writing to the young church in Corinth (1 Corinthians 2.16). Again it wasn't mere wishful thinking on his part; on the contrary, it was based on the promises of Christ regarding the Holy Spirit. 'When the Spirit of truth comes, he will guide you into all the truth... he will glorify me, because he will take what is mine and declare it to you' (John 16.13–14). These and similar promises were fulfilled at Pentecost when God sent his Spirit upon the Church, transforming ordinary men and women into Spirit-filled ambassadors for Christ.

God, as he had promised, hadn't left them in the dark, as it were, struggling along trying to make sense out of life. They were filled with wisdom and power that enabled them to know and do his will. God had given them his Spirit not to make up for the absence of Jesus, but to intensify the presence of Jesus. They became conscious of Christ being closer than ever before, teaching, informing and guiding them by his Spirit. They had the mind of Christ.

One of the most beautiful hymns of the early church is introduced with the same theme – a theme that is given substance in the sublime content of the hymn itself:

> Let the same mind be in you that was in Christ Jesus,
>   who, though he was in the form
>   of God
>   did not regard equality with God
>   as something to be exploited,
>   but emptied himself,
>   taking the form of a slave,
>   being born in human likeness.
>   And being found in human form,
>   he humbled himself
>   and became obedient to the point of
>   death –
>   even death on a cross.
>   Therefore God also highly exalted him
>   and gave him the name
>   that is above every name,
>   so that at the name of Jesus
>   every knee should bend,
>   in heaven and on earth and under
>   the earth,
>   and every tongue should confess
>   that Jesus Christ is Lord,
>   to the glory of God the Father.
>   (Philippians 2.5–11)

In this majestic hymn, which also formed part of the Church's early creed, we are given an incredible insight into the mind of Jesus. He shows us what being divine really means. He doesn't exploit it to his own advantage but willingly and humbly becomes human, partaking in a shameful death. He reveals his divine nature by being obedient to the divine will and going to his death on the cross. That's why God exalted him and made him Lord of all. He was lifted up on the cross to die, and he was lifted up in the resurrection and at the ascension to reign over all.

Paul's hymn is glorious, containing the kernel of the gospel of God, revealing the thinking of the mind of Christ and displaying the divine economy of life. By giving we receive, by serving we are served, by losing our life we find it, by humbling ourselves we are exalted. But the point of this sublime, high-flown theology is not for its own sake, but for our sake and for the sake of all who would follow the Christian way. By it we are encouraged to emulate the attitude and to mirror the mind of Christ. For if we have the mind of Christ we, like him, will be humble, obedient to the will of God and willing to suffer for it.

What a wonderful encouragement this is to offer our mind afresh to God each day, praying that through the power of the Holy Spirit his thoughts will become our thoughts, his ideas our ideas, his ways our ways.

6
Will

Bill and Desmond were both strong-willed, which made them excellent, if exasperating, members of the pastoral team. When a clear decision was called for, Bill was eager to make it as soon as possible. Desmond was the opposite. If the decision wasn't needed for another two hours, he wouldn't make it until thirty seconds before the deadline. He would then agree with Bill and be just as firm in his decision.

They were an invaluable combination. Each expressed his will strongly and each was true to himself. Procrastination was foreign to Bill's temperament; his motto was 'Grasp the nettle and get on with it'. If the matter was important he wanted action. Desmond, on the other hand, was like a dog with a bone, worrying away at the issue, asking questions and seeking more information right up to the last minute. If the matter was important he wanted to get it right.

Character in action

The manner in which Bill and Desmond acted in expressing their will was totally consistent with their character. Indeed, the will has been defined as character in action.

Our will does not operate on its own; it is part and parcel of the whole person. The Bible doesn't divide us into separate bits, like intellect, will, emotions, heart and mind. They are presented as overlapping categories representing the whole person. The human will is that collection of purposes and desires that both shape and reflect a person's character, choices and actions.

Though we are not always conscious of it, our will is functioning throughout the course of every day, articulating our desires, revealing our understanding of situations, and our purposes concerning them. For instance, when we take a trip, we do so in order to see a friend, to do some business or perhaps to have a holiday. Our mind sees the connection between actions and purpose. Even actions such as eating and sleeping, which have a built-in purpose based on bodily needs, become part of our overall system of desires, purposes and choices.

Our will matters. It is a vital part of our personal being, with an important contribution to make to the integrity of our relationship to the world, to other people and to God. Wrong choices, foolish desires or false ambitions can so easily spell disaster and cast a blight over the whole of life, not only for us but also for others.

Some have had their careers wrecked, their family life undermined and their health destroyed by wrong moral choices and selfish desires. Others, reaping the benefits of wise choices and purposeful activity, have achieved the so-called 'good life' – usually associated with material prosperity. Most of us, however, muddle through, sometimes getting it right, either through accident or design, and at other times getting it wrong, but always learning from our mistakes and developing our character as a result.

It all emphasizes the importance of the will and our need to recognize the teaching of scripture, that sin has brought disorder to the harmony and function of the whole person, including the will. If our heart and mind has not been renewed by the Spirit of God, then there is the possibility that false goals and desires will dominate our will, with disastrous results. But, as we saw in the previous two chapters, if we are being transformed in heart and mind by the Spirit of God, our will, in its choices and actions, should increasingly reflect that renewed character. Though, to be honest, this is not always the case.

Tug of war

There are times when even those who have the mind of Christ make wrong choices, nurture foolish desires and pursue false goals. If that were not so, the teaching contained in some of the New Testament letters would be unnecessary.

All was not well in the church at Philippi, for instance. Great personal differences had arisen out of rivalry, vanity, selfishness and animosity – including two women who were at loggerheads. Euodia and Syntyche were undoubtedly committed to the work of the gospel, but the disagreement between them was of such intensity as to cause harmful division in the church. Paul, therefore, had to encourage them to be united (Philippians 1.27; 2.2–4; 4.2). Even Peter and Paul, both of whom were strong-willed characters, had a major dust-up over a matter vital to the unity of the Church and progress of the gospel (Galatians 2.11). Paul even admitted to a tug-of-war going on within himself that threatened to hinder the work of God (Romans 7.14–25).

There is nothing unusual about conflict of this kind. Indeed we have been told to expect it. It is not necessarily a mark of regression but often it is a sign of growth. It is true that those who are in Christ have been made new, but it doesn't always feel like it, and it certainly doesn't happen all at once. We grow gradually into the likeness of Christ, and growth always carries an element of pain and struggle. Conflict within the life of the Christian is not an indication that the Holy Spirit is absent; it is much more likely to be the evidence of his presence.

When Christ imparts his new nature – what Paul called the Spirit – to us, he doesn't throw out our old nature – what Paul called the flesh. Flesh and Spirit, old and new, exist side by side. It is true that as we keep in step with the Spirit, and respond to his guidance and prompting, our old nature will diminish in power. Nevertheless, the Christian possesses two natures – old and new, flesh and Spirit – and the conflict between them is both fierce and unremitting (Galatians 5.16–25).

There are times, therefore, when we may feel like the handkerchief tied to the centre of the rope in a tug-of-war. We are being pulled first one way and then the other. Sometimes our heart rules our head, and vice versa, and at other times our self-will rushes ahead of them both and plunges us into a crisis we could well do without.

Most of us will have painful memories of occasions when we have wilfully rushed ahead of the Spirit and got ourselves into an embarrassing mess. One such occasion is indelibly seared on my memory. It happened on a train going from Euston to Heysham. I was on my way home to Belfast, having just been accepted to serve as a lay evangelist in London. In the circumstances, it seemed right to put my new-found status into practice and evangelize the passengers in my carriage. So I launched straight into the task – in my own strength and, on reflection, for a false motive, namely, self-justification. My selfish will took no heed of my heart nor my head. I listened neither to the people in the carriage nor to the Spirit within me, but only to my old selfish nature. The result was disastrous. I was going to Heysham but found myself 'sent to Coventry' before I reached Watford. Since those were the days before corridor trains, I was imprisoned for five hours with the evidence of my foolishness and failure. It was a long journey!

A guiding principle

Life, too, is a journey, and like most other journeys benefits from having a sense of direction, a destination to aim for, and a guiding principle to keep us going, especially when the going gets tough.

The Christian journey is no different, though its direction, destination and guiding principle may seem strange, if not foolish, to many people. But from start to finish, and all along the way, the matter of the will is crucial. The journey begins when we willingly respond to the call of Jesus to 'Follow me'. It continues as we willingly walk in his footsteps, hearing his word, obeying his teaching and following his example. It will end on the day when God wills to draw all things to himself. On that day creation will be healed, we shall know even as we are known, and heaven, where 'God is all in all', will be our home.

For Christians, the guiding principle of that journey is the will of God. 'Your will be done, on earth as it is in heaven' (Matthew 6.10), is not only a prayer taught by Jesus to his disciples and used by Christians across the centuries. It has also become a way of life for those who are serious about following the way of God.

But, though the scriptures provide us with a wealth of information as to the ways and purposes of God, deciding what the will of God is in specific circumstances can often prove difficult. Of course, there are times when it may be as clear as crystal. If a friend is in need, for instance, there would be little justification for us to turn our backs. But there are many other occasions when the will of God is anything but clear. Sometimes, even though we have prayed for guidance, it is only after we have taken a decision or embarked on a course of action that we receive the confirmation that it was indeed the will of God.

The fact remains, however, that for the Christian the guiding principle of life is to discover the will of God and to do it.

It was a way of life exemplified by the mother of Jesus. She responded, with unreserved readiness, to a call that was unique in human history. In giving her consent to bear in her womb the Messiah of God, she expressed her willingness to receive God's gift and be part of God's plan. In expressing her own will, she offered herself in complete obedience to the will of God. 'Here am I, the servant of the Lord, let it be to me according to your word.' In other words, 'Your will be done.'

She was the forerunner of countless disciples of Jesus who have chosen the will of God to be their guiding principle in life.

Yours or mine

Mary's eager response, which was, in essence, a statement of faith, makes it clear that she was not being forced to do God's will. This is both a wonderful and a terrifying truth. God does not force us to do his will. He respects our right to choose, even though he may sometimes disagree with the choice we make.

For instance, there is no greater power than the love of God – yet it can be spurned, as that sad comment in the prologue of John's Gospel makes clear: 'He came to what was his own, and his own people did not accept him' (John 1.11). Far from God expelling people from his presence, his people were the ones who were guilty of expulsion. His tears over Jerusalem were not produced by self-pity at being rejected, but by genuine sorrow that, in rejecting him, they were forgoing the peace they needed and bringing judgement upon their nation (Luke 19.41–44).

Even those twin commandments, that we should love God with all our heart and soul and mind and strength, and our neighbour as ourselves, require a willing response from us. Ultimately, our love towards God and towards people becomes a matter of the will – expressing the conviction of our whole person. We can offer or we can withhold our love and practical service.

I was reminded of this fact of life by the antics of one of my children in a simple and humorous incident by the seaside. When he was eighteen months old we took my son to play on a beach of very fine silvery sand. We watched, fascinated, as he plunged his hand into the sand and came up with a fist full which he then began to squeeze. But his chubby little hand couldn't quite manage it, and the tighter he tried to squeeze the faster the sand ran out. He was left with an empty hand and a mystified expression on his face. He tried it again and the same thing happened.

The third time, by pure coincidence of course, unless he gets his brains from his mother rather than his father, he picked up a handful of sand but didn't squeeze it. Instead, he held it in his tiny open palm and clearly enjoyed it. So did we, for unknowingly he had discovered a profound principle of life.

If we clasp our life tightly and selfishly to ourselves, we will lose it. If we open our life to God and to others, we shall find it (see Mark 8.35). If we say of our life, this is mine, I will do with it what I will, hands off, God will respect our choice but the outcome may be disappointing, if not disastrous. If on the other hand we acknowledge that we have received our life from God, and willingly place it in his hands to use as he wills in the service of his kingdom, the outcome will be different but demanding.

For if the example of Christ is anything to go by, we mustn't expect a life of calm tranquillity, but one of purposeful struggle and deep fulfilment. And, after all, it is his example we go by!

Yours not mine

The Christian's motivation to do God's will springs from the example of Jesus Christ, whose life and work was anchored in the will of God. Indeed his earthly ministry could be summed up as 'obedience in action'. Time and time again he explained that his deepest desire, the hunger of his soul, lay in doing the will of his Father. Though, to be frank, his own disciples often didn't understand the 'hunger' that motivated him.

On one occasion, when his disciples were urging him to eat something, he replied, 'I have food to eat that you do not know about.' They were a bit put out by this reply. Having obtained food for Jesus in the local village, they were puzzled that someone else may have supplied him. 'Surely no one has brought him something to eat?' they said to one another. At this Jesus made his famous comment, 'My food is to do the will of him who sent me and to complete his work' (John 4.31–38).

Jesus hungered to do the will of God to the very utmost, that is, until it was finished. While on earth Jesus wasn't on a three-year ego trip, creating an image and building a reputation for himself. His vocation was clear: 'I seek to do not my own will but the will of him who sent me.' He was committed to complete the work his Father had given him (John 5.30, 36). It is significant that his final words from the cross, before he laid down his life, were 'It is finished' (John 19.30). He had fulfilled his Father's will to the utmost. There were no loose ends, nothing left undone.

But it wasn't always a soft option, even for Jesus. His Gethsemane experience made clear that to be in the centre of God's will isn't always a comfortable place to be. The word Gethsemane itself derives from the Hebrew and Aramaic word for an olive-press used for crushing the olives to produce the oil so vital to the ancient economy. In the Garden of

Gethsemane Jesus felt crushed at the prospect of Calvary, so much so that the sweat stood out on his forehead and fell like great drops of blood to the ground. Here was sorrow, it seemed, beyond human comprehension.

Yet, in the midst of it Jesus said his glorious 'Yes' to God. 'Abba, Father, for you all things are possible; remove this cup from me; yet, not what I want, but what you want' (Mark 14.36). In seeking to do the will of God, Jesus, in his humanity, was not spared the agony of confusion and uncertainty. It was the struggle caused by the human will of Jesus intruding itself upon the will of God.

We need to remember that when we are facing our Gethsemane, for Gethsemanes there will be, if we follow our Lord's example of self-giving love. There will be times of doubt, fear and uncertainty, as we wrestle with doing the will of God in the midst of a complex world. He was not just the victim of either a humanly contrived crime or a cruel divine compulsion. He said, 'No one takes [my life] from me, but I lay it down of my own accord' (John 10.18). It was the divine compulsion of love that took him to the cross and explains the dignity and serenity that he showed there, in the face of betrayal, beatings, insults and the ignominious end to his unique life.

Jesus had options and so shall we, but in such circumstances the easy option is rarely the right one. Courage, based on obedience and trust, is required. Jesus admitted his fear, 'Father, remove this cup from me,' and acknowledged his trust and obedience: 'Yet, not what I want, but what you want.'

I believe that the victory of the cross was won in Gethsemane. Having said his 'Yes' to the will of God in the Garden, God said his 'Yes' to Jesus by raising him from the dead, placing him at his right hand and giving him the name above every name.

The will of God may sometimes be hard to discover and even more difficult to do. Nevertheless, the example of Jesus encourages us to keep trying, for the will of God is his character of incredible love in action. He wants only what is best for us. That should give us confidence to place our will in his.

7
Friends, neighbours, enemies

Since we were married my wife and I have moved house twelve times. Each time, before the removal van arrived, we had to make a choice as to what we dumped in the rubbish skip and what we took with us. Human nature being what it is, we wanted to dump or keep different things, so most of our rubbish went with us. But we did agree that one thing above all others must go with us – our address book. It was important that wherever we went, we kept in touch with our friends.

There is a very good reason for this. What we are like as people owes a great deal to the influence of other people and especially to our friends, our neighbours and, to some extent, our enemies.

The Bible makes it clear that relatedness is fundamental to our human nature. It is part of what it means to be made in the image of God. We are set in a network of human relationships, and our character grows towards maturity as we relate to and rub shoulders with other people in the daily process of living. We are who we are only in relation to others: to our parents, our children, our colleagues, our friends, our neighbours, our enemies, our society, our God.

For instance, I am a husband to my wife, a father to my children, a grandfather to my grandchildren and an uncle to my nephews and nieces. I was the Bishop of Bradford to the people in West Yorkshire and Bishop of Southwark to those in south London, but to my current neighbours I am the man with the springer spaniel who lives at number thirty!

Rich material

Above all, wherever I am, I remain a disciple of Jesus Christ, following in his footsteps and trying to relate purposefully to those, including my friends, neighbours and enemies, who impinge upon my daily life and play a part in my continued growth as a person.

It is for that reason that I constantly thank God for them. They form part of the network of relationships in which I have been set. They and I together are the rich material for the building of relationships that mirror the creative love of God, from which all love springs. We need, therefore, to pay attention to those relationships. We need to nurture and sustain them and, when broken, heal and restore them. The one thing we must not do is take them for granted. Adrian and Thomas did that, and brought great unhappiness upon themselves and others.

Their personal friendship led to the setting up of a business partnership that produced a flourishing commercial enterprise employing a score of people. The pressures of competition were fierce but they rose to the challenge, worked all the hours God gave them, and kept their business prosperous.

They didn't, however, work quite so hard at sustaining their friendship. Adrian, who first mooted the suggestion of business partnership, began to presume on their friendship and take crucial decisions without consulting Thomas. What was even worse, he lied, publicly declaring that Thomas had endorsed such decisions. It was a betrayal not only of friendship but also of trust. It led to the breakdown of friendship and the break-up of partnership. They set up rival firms and caused redundancies among their original workforce. Sadly, Adrian and Thomas didn't just become competitors, they became enemies.

Forgetting or neglecting our friends may be in a different league from betraying them, but nevertheless it brings its own feelings of guilt and regret. I recall listening to a senior church leader being interviewed towards the end of his working life.

'If you had your time over again,' said the interviewer, 'is there anything you would do differently?' The church leader was an honest man. He didn't waffle or blandly declare that he wouldn't change a thing, thus revealing that he had learnt nothing. Instead he firmly replied, 'Yes. I have been so busy working for God and the church that I have neglected my friendships. If I had my time over again, I would not make the same mistake.'

It was a poignant reminder that we must not take for granted those relationships in which we are set. We need to be sensitively aware of their nature and do all in our power to maintain, support and strengthen them. The scriptures offer us some help and guidance in this matter of nurturing and affirming.

Like one of the family

There are friends and there are friends. Our address book may be full of the names of our friends, many of whom have been influential in our lives, yet we know it would be almost impossible for us to maintain a consistently close and meaningful friendship with all of them. A card at Christmas or on a birthday is one thing, but a close personal friendship is not always possible or practicable. We remain friends but not close friends.

There is nothing unusual about this. The Bible word for friend can refer to anything from 'neighbour' to a distant acquaintance. The context determines the meaning. But the writer of Proverbs maintains that a few close friends are better than a multitude of acquaintances, and are in a class by themselves, a point which seems to be endorsed by our Lord's relationship with his 'beloved disciple' (John 13.23).

Proverbs has quite a bit to say about friends of one kind or another. The writer is scathing, for instance, about fair-weather friends, those whose friendships have strings attached. 'What's in it for me?' is their main concern, and usually the answer is wealth and influence. 'Wealth brings many friends, but the poor are left friendless... everyone is a friend to a giver of gifts' (Proverbs 19.4, 6).

By contrast, the close friend is like one of the family: 'Some friends play at friendship but a true friend sticks closer than one's nearest kin' (Proverbs 18.24). We know exactly what the writer means, for we all have friends who, even if circumstances have prevented us from meeting for years, can slot back naturally into the family circle and pick up where we left off, months or years before!

'A friend loves at all times' (Proverbs 17.17). These friends remain constant, whether in triumph or in tragedy. Aware of our faults and failings, their love is never withdrawn. They don't close their eyes to our shortcomings nor flatter us with half-truths. The reality of their friendship is measured by their honesty. They are faithfully frank – even if it hurts. 'Well meant are the wounds a friend inflicts, but profuse are the kisses of an enemy' (Proverbs 27.6).

My mentor as a young Christian was a blind clergyman who became, in the biblical sense of the word, a good friend. He had that extra awareness of people and situations that is so often the case with those who are blind, and had an amazing ability to comfort and to challenge. He would be reassuring, as true friends need to be, affirming what is good and commendable. But, unerringly and with understanding, he would put his finger, as it were, on the sore spots of one's life and expose that which needed help and healing. Time spent with him was never bland but always bracing. It had the integrity of true friendship.

It also had a built-in incentive. It made me determined to guard it with thoughtfulness and care, and to aim for the same integrity in my friendship with others. A good friend is a precious gift. So also is a good neighbour.

Beyond the family

However, we must not limit the term 'neighbour' to those who live next door or in the same street. Here we are not thinking so much about the closeness of family as an open neighbourliness that stretches much further afield and across cultural, racial and religious boundaries. The biblical meaning of 'neighbour' is twofold.

At one level, 'neighbour' refers to anyone in need, especially those with whom we come into contact. Such people were in mind when God said, 'You shall love your neighbour as yourself' (Leviticus 19.18) – words quoted on several occasions by Jesus in the Gospels. Indeed, he joined together our love for God and our love for our neighbour (Matthew 22.34–40). They are parallel and inseparable. We can't have one without the other. Our love for God is expressed in our love for other people. A failure to offer practical love to a neighbour in need is a failure of love towards God. This is particularly pertinent in those areas of our society and our world where basic human rights are ignored and injustice is rampant. Love towards our neighbour in such circumstances will mean confronting injustice and acting against all that diminishes human dignity.

This brings us to the second level of meaning as taught in scripture, namely that we become neighbours ourselves as we reach out in compassion to meet the needs of others.

This second meaning was dramatically illustrated by Jesus in his discussion with the lawyer that prompted his parable of the Good Samaritan (Luke 10.25–37). The lawyer had come to Jesus with the question, 'Teacher, what must I do to inherit eternal life?' Together they agreed that the keeping of the law was the right answer. 'You shall love the Lord your God with all your heart... and your neighbour as yourself.' But then came the real question that lay at the heart of the lawyer's concern: 'And who is my neighbour?'

In response, Jesus told the story of the man who was mugged and left seriously hurt on the roadside. A priest and a Levite, members of the Jewish religious establishment, saw him as they passed by, but refused to help. But when a Samaritan, an enemy of the Jews, saw the man, he responded with practical compassion. He gave him first aid on the spot, took him to a local inn and paid for his after-care!

Jesus concluded the story with a question to the lawyer that exploded his categories of thought. He had been examining the concept of 'neighbour' from a safe theoretical distance. He was concerned about definition. Being a good Jew, he wanted to draw a boundary-line that would indicate who was inside and who was outside the special love of God. He wanted to be properly selective and restrictive as to who his neighbour was.

Jesus, however, forced him to face the question from the perspective of the victim. The Jew lying injured on the roadside made the revolutionary discovery that the hated Samaritan was his neighbour and that his fellow Jews, the priest and the Levite, were not. As the parable unfolded, the lawyer's thinking was also turned upside down. He discovered that there was no boundary to be drawn. Neighbour love was to be unrestricted and non-selective.

So when Jesus asked him which person in the story is the 'neighbour' whom you are commanded to love as yourself, he surmounted the barrier of prejudice towards Samaritans and replied, 'The one who showed him mercy.' 'Go and do likewise,' said Jesus. In other words, go and be a neighbour, for the real question is not who is my neighbour, but rather, to whom am I a neighbour? Have I got the heart and mind and compassion of a neighbour? Am I prepared to be neighbourly, not only to my friends and neighbours but also to my enemies. And if need requires, am I also prepared to let them be a neighbour to me?

One step further

God's demands in these matters are quite startling. He insists that neighbourly love doesn't discriminate in favour of those who may deserve it. Christian love means doing good to those who have no intention of returning the compliment. We are to follow God's example. He lavished his gifts on the ungrateful. 'He is kind to the ungrateful and the wicked' (Luke 6.35).

But he went even further than that. To the commandment that we should love God and our neighbour as ourselves, was added a staggering, almost shocking, new requirement, namely, that we should love our enemies. It was revolutionary in its newness. 'You have heard that it was said, "You shall love your neighbour and hate your enemy." But I say to you, Love your enemies and pray for those who persecute you' (Matthew 5.43–44). Christ did exactly that when he prayed for those who were putting him to death. 'Jesus said, "Father, forgive them; for they do not know what they are doing"' (Luke 23.34). Such love, which knows no boundaries, will reflect the generosity of God himself. 'God proves his love for us in that while we still were sinners Christ died for us' (Romans 5.8).

Christ loved his enemies and so must we. But it isn't easy, nor is it always possible if we think of love only in emotional terms. When faced with bitter enmity and open hostility, the last thing we might feel for our enemies is love. On such occasions we must resort to what has been called 'willed love'. That is, we must, with an act of the will, do such good things as will benefit those who oppose us. Jesus taught us that the right way to counter hostility was to respond with an 'aggressive love'.

> If anyone strikes you on the right cheek, turn the other also; and if anyone wants to sue you and take your coat, give your cloak as well; and if anyone forces you to go one mile, go also the second mile.
>
> (Matthew 5.39–41)

It all seems so far removed from the reality of the world as we know it today, but nevertheless it may shock us out of our unthinking acceptance of the status quo. If we can begin, even in a small way, to return compassion for hate, to keep ourselves from giving way to uncontrolled anger, to turn the other cheek when verbally abused and give freely of our time and possessions, it could make a difference. If we can pursue these things with integrity, it could help to defuse conflict, disarm enmity and heal broken relationships.

No need to walk alone

Part of our love for friends, neighbours and enemies includes the duty and privilege of praying for them. This ought not to be seen as an 'optional extra' – a nice thing to do when you remember – but rather a purposeful act of love and goodwill that carries them, with us, into the larger context of the presence of God.

I vividly recall a retreat address by Archbishop Michael Ramsey, in which he spoke of the Ephod worn on the breasts of the high priests of Israel. It was an ornate and intricately woven garment containing two stones, on which were carved the names of the sons, or twelve tribes of Israel. Its symbolism was clear. The high priest bore the people on his heart when he came into the presence of God. 'So Aaron shall bear the names of the sons of Israel in the breastpiece of judgement on his heart when he goes into the holy place, for a continual remembrance before the LORD' (Exodus 28.29).

This illustration from the scriptures became a source of inspiration to me for my subsequent ministry. At the time of the retreat in question, I had just begun a new job which committed me to a fragmented lifestyle in which I lived out of a suitcase and travelled hundreds of miles each week. Once a week I touched base in a parish church and celebrated a Holy Communion service. As I stood before the altar, I found myself consciously bearing on my heart the names of people and places, sorrows and joys, that had made up my fragmented life in the previous week. In a quite remarkable way it brought a sense of integration and wholeness to my peripatetic ministry.

It is a practice that I have followed ever since, and in a manner that is not restricted to professional clergy but open to all people.

It came about when, following a serious heart attack, I was advised to walk five miles every day. I decided to make virtue out of necessity. A small notebook that slipped easily into my pocket contained the names of the many priests and parishes for which I, as bishop, had a special care. Each day as I left home to walk, I turned a page of the notebook on which was written the names of those for whom I would pray during the next hour and a half. Little did my colleagues know I was taking them for a walk! But it was a walk with intent. I didn't recite prayers as I went – I needed all my breath for walking – but I recalled their faces, families and parishes, and simply held them with me, in thought and prayer, within the love of God.

Habit dies hard. Today, though I don't walk quite so much, I never walk alone. Nor, indeed, do I ever go to church alone. It seems natural to carry specific friends, neighbours, and yes, even enemies, with me into the presence of God. The vicar's congregation is even larger than he thinks!

It would be easy to underestimate the impact and influence our friends and neighbours, and those who make our life difficult, have upon us. Under God they form an important part of our growth as persons on the way to maturity in Christ. We need to give thanks and pray for them. They are to be valued and loved. At the same time, we need to offer ourselves to God, that through our love and practical compassion we may assist and encourage them in their journey towards maturity, that together we may increasingly become the persons God intends us to be.

8
Past

'One of the reasons why old people make so many journeys into the past is to satisfy themselves that it is still there.' So wrote Ronald Blythe in his book *The View in Winter*. It was a perceptive, if selective, comment. The speed of change in our present world is so great, it is not surprising that some older people return to the past and revisit familiar waymarks to guide them through life's contemporary complexities.

It is true, of course, that many older people do have a tendency to refer to the past, and I can visualize the winks, nods and smiles exchanged between my children as they hear their father recall former glories for the umpteenth time! But older people are not the only ones who journey to the past. Wise people of every age return there in order that they may understand the present and find hope for the future. Far from being dead and gone, the past is alive with potential, instruction, incentive and, strangely enough, danger.

Prejudging the past

Danger was certainly what William (later Lord) Whitelaw had in mind when, at his first press conference after his appointment as Secretary of State for Northern Ireland, he said, 'I have always said it is a great mistake to prejudge the past.'

It sounds a bit Irish – as well it might, given his audience – but, in that particular context, it made a great deal of sense. In a society that for decades has been blighted by sectarian division, the past is often determined by whatever history book you read. Some sections of that society are forever returning to the past, and others give the impression that they have never left it. They are imprisoned by it. Therein lies the danger, and the cause of so much sectarian conflict in recent years, so that a healing of past memories may be that community's greatest need.

It was also Deborah's greatest need. The wife of a retired cardiologist, she served as a voluntary helper in the chaplaincy team of a large hospital. She won the confidence of the staff and was wonderful with the patients. Each week she would spend hours preparing the chapel, arranging the flowers, washing the linen and polishing the silver for the altar. Then, on Sunday morning, she would help bring the patients in wheelchairs to the Holy Communion service.

Deborah was indispensable, but at the same point in every service she became invisible. She left the chapel just as I began to distribute the bread and wine, returning only to take the patients back to the ward. It puzzled me, because I knew she was at the very least a nominal Christian. Gently, I raised the matter with her and discovered that she was imprisoned by her own prejudgement of the past. Guilty of a fairly serious moral lapse when she was in her early twenties, she felt ashamed and excluded from the church. Such was her temperament that she had never really talked about it to anyone, but presumed that such behaviour placed her, as it were, 'beyond the pale'. She sincerely believed that she was unfit to receive the sacramental body and blood of Christ.

It was one of the saddest moments of my ministry to discover that someone whose life was so exemplary felt shut out from the love of God in this way. It became one of the happiest moments of my ministry when, with a growing awareness of the teaching of scripture, she discovered the joy of being wrong. She came to know and understand that there was grace beyond regret, and faith beyond failure. Our Lord's generous attitude and forgiving spirit towards those guilty of moral failure – not only the woman taken in adultery (John 8.3–11), but also Peter in his desertion and threefold denial of Jesus (Matthew 26.69–75) – became a source of reconciliation and renewal. She continued to bring patients to receive Holy Communion, but now she also received the sacrament.

Redeeming the past

Deborah discovered that the past, which had imprisoned her, could be redeemed. Throughout the centuries of Christianity, multitudes have made the same discovery, often after years of unrelieved guilt.

One of the enormous privileges and responsibilities of being a priest is being invited to share people's sorrows and joys, to experience with them the highs and lows of life and especially to walk alongside them in their times of trouble and emotional stress. On such occasions it is the past, which has been shut up tightly inside them, that frequently comes to the surface and cries out for help and healing.

People don't always know how to deal with the past. Some create an imaginary past, drawing a veil over the unpleasant bits and glamorizing the good things. Some manipulate the past to justify their present, and perhaps unsavoury, way of life, while others simply live in the past, too afraid to let it go in case they lose their identity and sense of direction in the midst of a rapidly changing society.

Many, however, are aware that their past is in need of repair and some feel it requires a major transplant. They are conscious that old hurts have not been healed, that bitter words have not been withdrawn and apologies offered nor received. They remember sins neither confessed nor forgiven, jealousies neither acknowledged nor discarded, deceits not discovered and lies not admitted. They know the past is gone but it is certainly not dead. On the contrary, it rises up to haunt them and is a powerful and, at times, inhibiting influence on their present life. They know that they can't put the clock back but, somehow, they long to have the past put right.

That is a very natural human desire. It is also the desire of God – and he has done something wonderful about it. He has put right the past. That was the purpose of his love in sending Jesus into the world, and it was made clear from the outset, even before he was born. The message of the angel of the Lord to Joseph regarding Mary was, 'She will bear a son, and you are to name him Jesus, for he will save his people from their sins' (Matthew 1.21).

Without the saving help of Jesus Christ, men and women were no match for sin. They lived under its shadow and could not break free from its power. But the wonderful work of God through the cross and resurrection of Jesus changed all that. It broke the power of sin and death and provided new life for all those who trusted in Christ. The IOU, as it were, that was against them was not just cancelled, it was taken away and nailed to the cross. This truth was graphically declared by Paul when he described the new status of those who were in Christ: 'God made you alive together with him, when he forgave us all our trespasses, erasing the record that stood against us with its legal demands. He set this aside, nailing it to the cross' (Colossians 2.13–14).

Through the death and resurrection of Jesus Christ, God has dealt with the past. This is not just a pious thought held by the few, it has become the practical experience of countless disciples of Jesus across the ages, beginning with those gathered behind the closed doors of a house in Jerusalem on the first Easter evening. As a group they were totally demoralized. Not only was their future bleak, their past was in tatters. The one in whom they had put their trust had been rejected and crucified. What was even worse, they were filled with guilt, shame and a sense of moral failure that they had deserted and abandoned him. They were in a tragic vacuum.

But into that vacuum came the risen Jesus. 'Jesus came and stood among them and said, "Peace be with you." After he said this, he showed them his hands and his side. Then the disciples rejoiced when they saw the Lord' (John 20.19–20). There were no words of rebuke from Jesus, no extraction of a promise from them to do better next time, no strings attached regarding either the past or the future. His very presence was forgiveness. As a result, and with the help of the Holy Spirit, they were able to rewrite their lives, including their past lives, from an entirely new perspective.

With the Holy Spirit's assistance, we can do the same. Jesus

Christ is Lord of all – including the past. Therefore, it need neither imprison nor inhibit us. It is forgiven. Nevertheless, there will be times when our memory recalls those things of which we are ashamed, and we will be tempted to despair. When that happens we need to recall what Jesus has done through his death and resurrection, and to follow the advice offered by Charity Lees Bancroft in her beautiful hymn:

> When Satan tempts me to despair
> and tells me of the guilt within,
> upward I look, and see him there
> who made an end of all my sin.

In Jesus Christ the past has been redeemed.

Gratitude for the past

But in Jesus Christ the past is also alive with potential, instruction and incentive. There is so much to be grateful for, and most of us, young or old, draw strength and inspiration from it. The past is not a nostalgic optional extra, as it were, for us to dip into from time to time. It is much more important than that. A proper view and interpretation of the past is vital to our understanding of the present, and there is a crucial connection between our memory of the past and our hope for the future. If we do not learn lessons from the past, we are liable to repeat old mistakes and create new and more complex problems.

The theologian Walter Brueggemann wrote, in an American context: 'Our consumer society is organized against history.' In other words, it undervalues the past and derides the future. There is what he called 'a depreciation of memory and a ridicule of hope.' His words have a pertinence to our own society where, in the eyes of many, the present is all that matters. The past is gone; the future, if there is a future, can take care of itself. As a result, our society, for all its affluence and pursuit of pleasure, often produces in people a sense of meaninglessness and hopelessness.

How important it is, therefore, that we guard against amnesia concerning the past. Of course there will be things that we are more than delighted to forget. For instance, a visit to the dentist today is usually a pleasant experience in comparison to what I remember of fifty years ago! We need to be honest about the past and not glorify it beyond all recognition. But we must not be dismissive of it, for our future hope will be, to some extent, shaped by the past.

In the very early days of our Christian ministry, my wife and I had to endure an experience, over a period of two years, when the circumstances surrounding us were so unbelievably demoralizing that we might have been put off Christianity for life. Instead, with the help of friends and wise Christian leaders, that wilderness experience proved to be remarkably formative for our subsequent life and ministry. We learned that God remains faithful. He does not abandon his people. The memory of that experience, and God's presence within it, has enabled us not only to face demanding challenges across five decades, but also to find joy and fulfilment in doing it, helped, unwittingly, by our children and grandchildren.

One of our devices for keeping our children occupied on wet Sunday afternoons when they were young was a box of old photographs. Much to our amusement, they found the hairstyles and clothes worn by their parents highly entertaining. Exclamations like, 'Will you look at that hat?', 'Do you see the length of that dress?' and 'How's that for a hairdo!' were followed with roars of laughter. We laughed with them, but at the same time we were transported into the past and reminded of so many people, places and events that shaped our lives, filled us with gratitude and gave us hope for the future.

Remember – don't forget

It is significant that God repeatedly warned his people not to forget the past. 'Take care that you do not forget the LORD, who brought you out of the land of Egypt, out of the house of slavery' (Deuteronomy 6.12). Indeed, he positively exhorted them to remember the past, and gave them symbols to help them, 'so that all the days of your life you may remember the day of your departure from the land of Egypt' (Deuteronomy 16.3).

God particularly wanted them to remember how they had been delivered from slavery. He had promised to do so and he kept his promise. It was this recollection of the faithfulness of God that sustained the hopes of the faithful when later Israel was carried into captivity and deprived of temple, monarchy and priesthood. It was also the memory of that past deliverance that nurtured hope in the hearts of people like Mary, Zechariah and Simeon (Luke 1.46–79; 2.25–39). They longed for and believed that the Messiah would come and bring an even greater deliverance than that foreshadowed in the Exodus.

Remarkably, when Jesus Christ, God's Messiah, was about to complete his earthly ministry and return to his Father, he gave his followers symbols to help them remember his life and his work of deliverance. Paul reminds us:

> The Lord Jesus on the night when he was betrayed took a loaf of bread, and when he had given thanks, he broke it and said, 'This is my body that is for you. Do this in remembrance of me.' In the same way he took the cup also, after supper, saying, 'This cup is the new covenant in my blood. Do this, as often as you drink it, in remembrance of me.' For as often as you eat this bread and drink this cup, you proclaim the Lord's death until he comes.
> (1 Corinthians 11.23–26)

The significance of these words is that they embrace the past, present and future. Through the symbols of bread and wine, the cross becomes 'energized'; that is, the cross not only belongs to the past but it has power to help form and reform what we are in the present. At the same time, it inspires us to be witnesses for Christ in the future, 'until he comes'. One of the post-communion prayers from the Anglican Communion Service sums it up beautifully and powerfully. Having received the sacrament of the body and blood of Christ, we thankfully and prayerfully respond:

> May we who share Christ's body live his risen life;
> we who drink his cup bring life to others;
> we whom the Spirit lights give light to the world.
> Keep us firm in the hope you have set before us,
> so we and all your children shall be free,
> and the whole earth live to praise your name;
> through Christ our Lord.

The Eucharist reminds us, as does Walter Brueggemann, that the Christian Church is rooted in energized memories and summoned by radical hopes.

Forget and press on

Without question Paul was summoned by radical hopes that motivated his mission to the gentile world. His description, above, of what Christians are doing when they 'break bread', is a clear indication that he was also rooted in energized memories. For him the past was alive with meaning and inspiration, together with some pain and perplexity, but he wisely kept it in perspective. Daringly, he suggested that there are times when we need to forget the past for the sake of the gospel.

Paul's all-consuming desire was to know Christ, but he admitted, when writing to the Philippians, that he had not yet reached that goal. He knew that Christ was too great to be grasped in a single lifetime, but he was determined to press on towards that goal. He said, 'This one thing I do: forgetting what lies behind and straining forward to what lies ahead, I press on towards the goal for the prize of the heavenly call of God in Christ Jesus' (Philippians 3.13–14). What on earth did he mean by 'forgetting what lies behind'? He couldn't possibly be suggesting an erasing of the memory when the central act of Christian worship was an act of remembrance, 'Do this in remembrance of me'. No, he was suggesting something vitally important.

Paul carried two great burdens, namely failure and success. He had persecuted the Church of Jesus Christ and he had a remarkably fruitful ministry as apostle to the gentiles. But he was determined that his pursuit of Christ and his mission would not be paralysed by past failures nor impeded by past successes. He knew that his great failure in persecuting Christ and his Church had been forgiven by the grace of God – his past was redeemed. He also knew that his achievements had been made possible only by that same grace of God. He felt convinced, therefore, that both failure and success could be put behind him in order that he could concentrate on one thing only – to finish the race, to reach the goal, to win the prize of knowing Christ as fully as Christ knew him. It is a classic example for all disciples of Christ to follow.

I return to where I began this chapter. Our past is full of potential. It can imprison and impede. It can inspire and encourage. Offered to God, the past can be redeemed, becoming a resource of experience to assist us in the present and provide us with a wellspring of hope for the future.

9
Present

I was sitting quietly in the House of Lords, minding my own business and sipping a glass of wine before dinner, when one of the noble lords moved purposefully towards me. The glint in his eye was unmistakably mischievous. Like me, he had escaped from a rather boring debate, and in order to pass the time before his meal he had decided to play 'bait the bishop' – and had me firmly in his sights.

'Now then, Bishop,' he said, 'how is it that you chaps are always going on about the past or the future but rarely about the present? You talk with great passion about events that took place two thousand years ago, and get excited about what is going to happen in that sweet by-and-by you call heaven. But what about the present? What about the here and now? What about today?' The noble lord had a point and I told him so, though I suggested that he had rather exaggerated in the interests of pre-prandial entertainment! The purposeful glint in his eye that I had noticed earlier became a twinkle as he graciously admitted his humorous intent.

Yet the concern expressed in his comments must not be dismissed, for we cannot exaggerate the formative nature of the present time. Today is the new reality that dawns every time the sun rises, and most of us are glad to welcome it. It represents a kind of new beginning and we are pleased to have a chance to make the most of it. While acknowledging the importance of both the past and the future, we are glad to accept the challenge of finding happiness and fulfilment amid the ordinary, awkward, contradictory contingencies of our present daily life.

This is as true of those who make no claim to faith as it is of those who do. It was certainly true of my friend the noble lord who, though he professed no particular faith, welcomed the opportunity that each new day brought for him to use his creative energy and experience in serving the needs of the physically handicapped. But it is also true of Christians, and perhaps more so because our belief in Christ as our contemporary fills the present with excitement and vitality.

The contemporary Christ

We believe that the present time is the forum for our Christian development and the backdrop against which our faith either flourishes or languishes, because it is also the sphere in which Christ is working through the power of his Spirit.

As we noted earlier, the Holy Spirit was given to the Church not to make up for the absence of Jesus but to intensify his presence among us. Jesus made this clear in his farewell address to his disciples:

> I still have many things to say to you, but you cannot bear them now. When the Spirit of truth comes, he will guide you into all the truth; for he will not speak on his own, but will speak whatever he hears, and he will declare to you the things that are to come. He will glorify me, because he will take what is mine and declare it to you. All that the Father has is mine. For this reason I said that he will take what is mine and declare it to you.
>
> (John 16.12–15)

We mustn't limit this promise to the life of the early Church. It has a universal application. The Holy Spirit makes Christ our contemporary in every age. In every age the Spirit is our living companion, teacher and helper, making known to us the mind of Christ in our present situation and guiding us regarding his purpose and will.

Like any good teacher, Jesus refused to pour into the minds of his first disciples more than they could contain. He knew that in the ages to come the Church would encounter unimaginable situations and challenges about which he had given no specific guidance. When that happened, it would be foolish simply to repeat some words of his spoken in an entirely different situation. Instead, they were to look to the Holy Spirit to guide them regarding the word of God that was pertinent to their immediate context.

It was a lesson I learned by being thrown in off the deep end when, in the early days of my Christian work, I was 'volunteered' to preach regularly in the open air. It was thrilling and terrifying to climb on to a soapbox at Speakers' Corner in Hyde Park or on Tower Hill. But it wasn't an edifying experience for those who listened, for on reflection I tended to string Bible texts together and fire them off in rapid succession hoping that some would hit the target. The trouble was, I didn't always identify the target! Not having 'listened' to the context of my hearers, I was scratching where people weren't itching. If I hit the target, it was by accident rather than design.

That is not true of the Holy Spirit. He doesn't miss the target. 'He speaks whatever he hears,' and reveals the things of Christ, who always hit the target. He was always on the wavelength of ordinary people, touching them where they were and at the deepest level. Small wonder multitudes flocked to hear him. That same creative Spirit makes that same Christ our contemporary today. 'Jesus Christ is the same yesterday and today and for ever' (Hebrews 13.8). He is not confined to first-century Palestine, nor held in reserve for a grand appearance at the final curtain. Through his Spirit he is intimately involved in the present. If he were not, there would be no present, for he is the sustainer of all things, including the present. 'He himself is before all things, and in him all things hold together' (Colossians 1.17). His presence guarantees the present and makes it alive with infinite possibilities.

This is the day

The fact that Jesus is Lord of the present as well as the past and future is a source of encouragement. We are not left alone. His promise, 'I am with you always, to the end of the age' (Matthew 28.20), holds good for us today. But his presence as the risen Lord not only brings us reassurance, it also inspires us to make the fullest and best use of the time available to us.

'What about today?' asked the noble lord. But frankly, that is the same question that Jesus has put to his followers in every age. He wouldn't let people off the hook by allowing them to dwell on the past or dream about the future. He was always bringing people back to the present moment, and their need to grapple with the realities of life today. The lawyer who had initiated, and was enjoying, a philosophical discussion about eternal life was told by Jesus to go and get on with being a good neighbour! (Luke 10.25–37). And when the demon-possessed man, having been healed by Jesus, begged to be allowed to stay with him, Jesus refused. Instead, he sent him home to face the realities of life in restoring relationships within his family and community (Mark 5.1–20).

It is true that in Christ our past is forgiven and our future is secure, but that commits us to live the forgiven life here and now and to forgive as we have been forgiven. It also requires us to anticipate the future by being visible signs of hope now, within all the complexities of life in the twenty-first century. We know, for instance, that one day Jesus will wipe away tears from every eye (Revelation 21.3–4), but metaphorically speaking that means getting out our handkerchiefs now. We must offer practical compassion and care to those who suffer today. The only time we have got is the present. This is the day of opportunity. We must 'seize the day'.

It was that kind of urgency that motivated Gordon to dedicate his free time to helping vagrants and rough sleepers on the streets of London. He was a complex character with no overt religious allegiance. Tactfulness was not high on his list of social graces, but he had a warm heart and a generous personality. His enthusiasm was so infectious that people rarely refused his request for help with food and clothing. Indeed, the standing joke among his colleagues was, 'If you don't look out, Gordon will have the suit off your back for one of his friends on the street.'

Homelessness, as far as Gordon was concerned, was a shameful comment on the life of our modern society. Not everyone agreed with the stance he took, and because his commitment was so passionate he sometimes lost old friends, who accused him of gullibility and fanaticism. But he also gained many new friends, for he didn't just talk about the problem of rough sleepers, he did something about it. He wasn't content simply to buy a copy of *The Big Issue*. He encouraged, some would say badgered, and inspired others to help him establish 'soup runs', where hot drinks, sandwiches and warm clothing were regularly on offer. He got close enough to his 'street friends' to know when they needed medical attention, and made arrangements for them to have it. He then went the extra mile by opening his home to them for a short period of after-care.

Gordon's service to the street people was a practical and emotional one, but it was founded on a solid moral and ethical base. While he might not have been a card-carrying member of any particular faith or church denomination, he believed that the sight of another human being rummaging in dustbins for food and sleeping rough on the streets was a rebuke to a civilized society. His work was also based on the conviction that 'tears needed to be wiped away today' – tomorrow may be too late. He seized the day.

Decisive moments

Gordon's sense of urgency about the present was not unique. It is shared by most of us from time to time. Normally life proceeds according to a daily routine and purpose that fluctuates between the mundane and the meaningful. But most of us have those special moments when the decisions we take have far-reaching consequences for the direction and ultimate significance of our life. The Bible uses two particular words in this connection. *Chronos* generally refers to so-called ordinary, or calendar, time. The word *kairos*, on the other hand, generally refers to those decisive moments that can change the course of life and determine the shape of the future. It is both interesting and instructive to note the way in which Jesus responded to calendar time and decisive, or special, time.

Though his public life and work lasted just under three years, most attention, quite properly, is focused on that particular period. Nevertheless, his thirty 'hidden years' in Nazareth are very important. Though Luke is the only biblical writer who tells us anything about his childhood, what he records is of deep significance. Jesus, thoughtlessly it seemed, brought grief to his human parents by being absent without leave during a visit to Jerusalem. They found him in the Temple, surprised by their anxiety: 'Why were you searching for me? Did you not know that I must be in my Father's house?' (Luke 2.49). Even at the age of twelve and in the process of life in calendar time, as it were, there was a *kairos*, or decisive, moment for Jesus as he publicly recognized God as his Father, and the priority of God's work.

Immediately afterwards, however, he returned to Nazareth with Mary and Joseph, remaining obedient to them. He 'increased in wisdom and in years, and in divine and human favour' (Luke 2.52). In other words, he developed an integrated personality; growing mentally, physically, spiritually and socially within the environment of an ordinary home and in calendar time.

Yet the period of his public ministry was the decisive time, not only for him but also for the nation of Israel and, ultimately, for the whole world. He gave a clear hint of this to his disciples when he said, 'We must work the works of him that sent me while it is day; night is coming when no one can work' (John 9.4). He was referring, of course, to his earthly mission for which he and his disciples would only have a limited time. Within a few months the storm clouds that were already circling around his head would burst at Calvary and overwhelm him in crucifixion and death.

Jesus was not taken by surprise. He recognized that this was the decisive moment, the very hour, for which he was born, and he refused to be deflected from it. As the time for his crucifixion came close, he said, 'Now my soul is troubled. And what should I say – "Father, save me from this hour"? No, it is for this reason that I have come to this hour' (John 12. 27). This was his *kairos* hour, the time determined by God, when the cosmic struggle between light and darkness would take place with Jesus as the victor. 'Now is the judgement of this world; now the ruler of this world will be driven out. And I, when I am lifted up from the earth, will draw all people to myself' (John 12.31–32).

But it was also the decisive moment for Israel. For centuries they had longed for their Messiah to come, but Jesus didn't match their preconceived image of Messiah, so they rejected and crucified him. Though a few welcomed and followed him, the majority, led by their religious leaders, failed to recognize that their decisive moment had come. It was their *kairos* time, when their response to the offer of God's peace would determine the shape of their future. They refused to recognize his person or receive his peace. Through their blindness and prejudice, they brought judgement upon their nation, 'because you did not recognize the time of your visitation from God' (Luke 19.44).

Getting it right

Most of us will be able to recall those special times in our own lives that have proved decisive and determinative, though sometimes it is only on looking back that we can identify them. But God works through the ordinary moments as well as the decisive ones. All of the present time is his gift to us and, like any other gift, needs to be received with gratitude and used creatively not only for our own fulfilment but also for the benefit of others.

It was Pope John XXIII who said, 'Do not walk through time without leaving worthy evidence of your passage' (Ward and Wild, 1997). That goal and ambition is not the prerogative of the rich and famous; it is within the reach of everyone, and many achieve it. There are those who are capable of 'painting on a larger canvas,' as it were. Coming from various walks of life, they have become household names because of their achievements at national or international level. But the fabric of our society would be the poorer if it were not for ordinary people who, by being good parents, teachers, lollipop persons, doctors, nurses, carpenters, shopkeepers, or any of a multitude of other occupations, provide worthy evidence of their passage through time.

Sarah is a fine example of what I mean. She sees life as a gift from God, even though she has cancer. Indeed, since the disease was diagnosed, the gift of life has become even more precious and not to be wasted. She regularly visits the sick and makes light of her own condition as she acknowledges, with a sensitive holding of a hand or a gentle touch on the brow, the suffering being endured by another. Her own experience of the disease seems to have equipped her with a special empathy with those similarly afflicted, and out of her own slowly deteriorating physical weakness she brings strength and courage to the weak. Sarah, like so many others who make a significant contribution to society, is unknown outside a rather small circle of people, but in their eyes the 'evidence of her passage through time' is immense and incontrovertible.

Steve stands in deep contrast to Sarah; there's nothing quiet, gentle or retiring about him. Wherever he is, his personality seems to cry out for attention. He simply can't be ignored. Those who are bemoaning the fact that something of importance can't be done are often interrupted by him doing it! He crowds more activity into one day than others do in a week. His Filofax is full to bursting point. But, and here is the point, his care of people, the strong as well as the weak, the rich as well as the poor, is outstanding. Busy he undoubtedly is, and to very good effect, but his priorities are such that he always seems accessible to those who need him most. He touches for good the lives of countless people, many of them made breathless simply by witnessing his energy and drive, and all of them grateful for the very clear and worthy evidence of his passage through time.

Sarah and Steve may stand in contrast, but they share a common conviction. They see the present as a gift from God and enjoy the rhythm of life with its highs and lows, mundane and meaningful. But, supremely, they see the present as a time of opportunity. They both believe that with Christ as their contemporary, through the power of his Spirit, they can make him visible through their lives of purpose and love. Though entirely different in personality and temperament, they are equally determined to make each day count. They don't waste the present by worrying about the future. They welcome it, are grateful for it, offer it back to God each day and, with his help, use it to the full. They seem to have got it right.

10
Future

'The future is not what it was.'

At first glance this may sound like a rather zany comment, but on examination it becomes an astute assessment of the way things are in our present world. Attributed to an anonymous professor of economics by Bernard Levin in the *Sunday Times* (22 May 1977), it highlights how the geography of the future can be drastically altered by events happening in the present. Those unfortunate people, for instance, whose savings and pensions have disappeared overnight because of the mismanagement or misdemeanour of others, would certainly agree that their future is not what it was.

All of us, however, would have to admit that the future is less predictable than it was fifty years ago, such has been the speed of change not only in the world of economics but also in the social fabric of our society. The old fashioned close-knit communities have largely broken down. Mobility and fragmentation are two of the characteristics of our day. People rarely spend a lifetime in one home or one job. Serial marriages are commonplace. Fewer people live and work in the same community, and when it comes to worship they tend to 'pick and mix' according to what is on offer and their own particular fancy.

Despite all this, or perhaps because of it, there is still a strong desire to plan and provide for the future. Though some would claim that a secure future is a contradiction in terms, the quite proper emphasis on obtaining a sound education is clearly directed at creating a stable, if not secure, future. And, though many would deny it, the popularity of the National Lottery is not just the excitement of watching and waiting for the number on the little coloured balls to appear, nor indeed the benefit to charities that will result. The thought of a massive win and, consequently, a secure future in material terms is a powerful incentive to buy a ticket.

Notwithstanding its unpredictability, most of us look to the future with a mixture of hope and realism. And those who have faith in God would also add a quiet confidence, based neither on arrogance nor on fantasy but on their trust in the loving purposes of their creator. They believe that the future, whatever shape it may take, is tied up with God and certainly not outside his control. Because of this, the future can be faced not with crippling fear but with a sense of awe and excitement, though on occasion mixed with a natural and realistic anxiety.

You can be too careful

It was about the nature of that anxiety that Jesus spoke so graphically in his famous Sermon on the Mount. He said some strange and challenging things, the essence of which may be summed up: 'So do not worry about tomorrow, for tomorrow will bring worries of its own. Today's trouble is enough for today' (Matthew 6.34). On the surface it appeared that Jesus was advocating carelessness regarding the future, a view seemingly endorsed by his other words, 'Do not worry about your life, what you will eat or what you will drink, or about your body, what you will wear' (Matthew 6.25).

Yet we know that he was not careless about the future. On many occasions he showed great concern for people's future welfare. For instance, even in the midst of the cosmic struggle on the cross, he showed concern for the future well-being of his mother and his beloved disciple. To Mary he said, 'Woman, here is your son', and to John he said, 'Here is your mother' (John 19.26–27). He had a similar concern about the future when feeding the four thousand. The motivation for the miracle was his compassionate concern that after three days travelling they might not get home safely. 'If I send them away hungry to their homes, they will faint on the way – and some of them have come a great distance' (Mark 8.3).

So when Jesus tells people not to worry nor be anxious, he is not recommending carelessness, he is warning them of the danger of being too full of care about the wrong things.

Every time I read these words of Jesus, I am reminded of Ian and Rita. I was thrilled when they asked me to prepare them for Confirmation and believed that, with their energy and enthusiasm, they would be a real gift to the local church. And so it proved – for two years. Then they unexpectedly inherited a considerable fortune, and everything changed. Far from releasing them from worry about the future, it burdened them with a chronic anxiety that destroyed their peace of mind and placed their Christian commitment on the back burner. It wasn't that they were overburdened with business responsibilities, they were simply over-anxious about maintaining and increasing their material wealth.

Some words of John Stott describe their situation perfectly; they were afflicted with 'a materialism which tethers our hearts to earth'. They had lost their bearings and with it their Christian perspective and sense of priority. They had also lost the ability to focus on such questions as: Just how much material wealth do you need to provide security for the future? Is not such security vulnerable in a world of change? Would it not be more Christlike to surrender most of it to the needs of the destitute in the Third World? Ian and Rita didn't deny their faith, and occasionally worshipped in their local church, but the 'cares of this world' had clearly choked their former enthusiastic Christian commitment (Mark 4.19).

It would be a mistake, however, to believe that Jesus was only interested in so-called spiritual things. Many of his parables and miracles and much of his teaching proclaim the opposite. He was deeply concerned about the basic material needs of people: bread for the hungry, water for the thirsty and clothing for the naked. Indeed, he declares that these things are so high on his list of priorities that he won't forget them. Since he has given us the supreme gift of life, he will not be remiss in providing the lesser gifts of food and clothing. After all, since he offers that service to the birds of the air and the flowers of the field, why should his care for us be any less? Besides, excessive worry doesn't prolong life – it tends to shorten it!

First things first

The real issue at stake here is getting our priorities right. Jesus put his finger on the spot when he said, 'Where your treasure is, there your heart will be also... No one can serve two masters... You cannot serve God and wealth' (Matthew 6.21–24). It is a fairly uncompromising statement! But the context of it reveals that Jesus is emphasizing that the absolute commitment of his disciples to follow him is to be matched by an absolute trust in God's faithfulness to provide them with the necessities of life. He hasn't forgotten the material needs of life, but the kingdom of God has the prior claim. Get that right and the other things will follow. We are to 'strive first for the kingdom of God and his righteousness, and all these things will be given to you as well' (Matthew 6.33).

It is this thought of the 'kingdom of God and his righteousness' that is so important for our assessment of and commitment to the future. Though there is a real sense in which the kingdom of God arrived with the coming of Christ, it is also true that it has yet to come in all its fullness. And so, as Jesus taught us to do, we continue to pray to God our Father, 'Your kingdom come. Your will be done, on earth as it is in heaven' (Matthew 6.10).

But we are not only to pray that way, we are also to live that way. God will bring in the fullness of the kingdom but we are expected to cooperate with him in that task. At its heart 'the kingdom of God' refers to the rule or reign of God. We 'seek first the kingdom of God and his righteousness' therefore, when God's will is paramount in our lives and we are committed to pursuing kingdom values, standards and priorities. That is not only God's right way of living; it is also a way in which he brings in the kingdom.

This, of course, has remarkable implications for the future. It brings the future into the present or, to put it another way, it enables us to live tomorrow's life today.

Professor Hans Küng described God's kingdom as 'Creation healed'. That certainly is a wonderful and inspiring vision of the future, but it doesn't require us to 'sit on our hands' and wait for it to happen. If we pray daily to God for his kingdom to come, we cannot opt out from the responsibility of becoming part of the answer to our own prayer. Rather, it requires us to anticipate the kingdom by what we are and what we do, to become mirrors that reflect glimpses of God's ultimate purpose for his creation. So, for instance, when we bring peace into situations of conflict, reconciliation into areas of division and love into places of hatred, then hurts are healed, the kingdom comes and we catch a glimpse of tomorrow's reality today.

The Catholic priest and Protestant minister in Northern Ireland who risked misunderstanding, ridicule and violence to hold a joint service on Maundy Thursday provided their local community with such a moving experience of the future. The service, recalling the night before the crucifixion of Jesus Christ, daringly included a symbolic act of foot-washing. As Protestants washed the feet of Catholics and Catholics washed the feet of Protestants, the kingdom of God drew near. Reconciliation began to be realized, barriers of prejudice began to be dismantled and unity in Christ was given visible expression. The future pressed back on to the present as, together, they caught a glimpse of God's ultimate purpose for the whole of his creation.

Pie in the sky?

To many people the thought that God has an ultimate purpose for the whole of creation is simply wishful thinking. As far as they are concerned, such sentiments are out of touch with reality. 'Pie in the sky when you die,' they would say. A future built on dubious speculation is a future built on sand. Hope of this nature, they would insist, is like whistling in the dark, a device to assuage our uncertainty and hide our fears.

We must be careful not to be dismissive of such people. Often their views arise out of a realism that is commendable, for there is so much in life that can lead to despair. It is reckoned, for instance, that at any one time there are thirty wars in progress around the world. The intractable problem of the Middle East, the growing famine areas of our world, which periodically burst upon our consciousness with dreadful scenes of starvation and death, and the increasing threat of global terrorism, can leave most of us with feelings of despair and impotence, together with genuine uncertainties about the future.

Besides, there are few of us who have not suffered from disappointed hopes, things that we would have liked to do, but one thing and another has prevented them from happening. Time has moved on, opportunities have gone and we are left with a feeling of what might have been. Most of us have been victims of false, tantalizing hope that offered so much and delivered so little. And haven't we all uttered those wistful words, 'I hope so,' when we have been anything but hopeful? As we think of the future, therefore, there is need for a realism that doesn't sweep the complexities, contradictions and disappointments of life under the carpet. Instead, we need to wrestle and work with such circumstances, and try to discern the seeds of hope and the signs of God's future breaking into the present. Humble faith regarding the future rather than arrogant certainty may be a healthier attitude to adopt.

Christian hope

Yet we must not ignore the fact that the scriptures have a vision of the future that is fostered neither by human optimism nor self-confidence. It is certainly not 'pie in the sky when you die'. On the contrary, it is based on a hope that is in touch with the real world of brokenness and pain, complexity and conflict. It doesn't offer soft answers but grapples with reality. It is a hope for the future rooted in the reality of God's faithfulness and God's future. It is a distinctively Christian hope – a hope that carries credibility because it was born and sustained within a context of hopelessness, uncertainty and frustration, where Christians were surrounded by persecution, suffering and fear.

It was in such circumstances that St Paul, inspired by the Holy Spirit, shared a remarkable vision of the future with the Christians in Rome, beginning with these words: 'I consider that the sufferings of this present time are not worth comparing with the glory about to be revealed to us' (Romans 8.18). He went on to speak of a freedom from decay in the whole creation and the glorious liberty of the children of God. (Romans 8.19–21). Though surrounded by apparent hopelessness, frustration and despair, Paul, with the eyes of faith, saw signs of a glorious future.

There are two key elements in Paul's conviction about the future. The first is his wonderful metaphor about birth, and the second is his teaching about the Holy Spirit.

He says, 'We know that the whole creation has been groaning in labour pains until now; and not only creation, but we ourselves, who have the first fruits of the Spirit, groan inwardly while we wait for adoption, the redemption of our bodies' (Romans 8.23). Paul's words graphically remind us of God's 'motherly' qualities. Giving birth is a wonderful metaphor of God's creative activity. And Paul, in the midst of the struggle, pain and frustration that were afflicting not only creation but also the Christian Church, does not despair, but instead discerns the labour pains of God's new creation. He uses the thought of labour pains as a sign of hope that there will be a new birth.

Of course, some of the 'groanings and sufferings' are related to God's judgement against what is wrong, but these need to be placed in the larger context of God bringing to birth new things: a new creation, a new people, a new humanity. God is making things new again, making things how they should be. This is all part of what Paul meant by the glorious freedom of both creation and the children of God (Romans 8.21).

The second element in Paul's conviction about the future is his teaching about the Holy Spirit. Indeed, the Holy Spirit is the principal reason why he can speak with such glorious assurance about the future. The life of the new creation, the life of liberty that God is giving his people, is the Holy Spirit. Of course, we are very far, yet, from the kingdom of God's glory. We have a long way to go. But Pentecost, which marks the coming of the Holy Spirit upon the Church and the world, reminds us that God has given us his Spirit as a guarantee that we are on the way. That's why Paul held such a firm hope in the future in the midst of an uncertain and unpromising environment. The word used by Paul of the Holy Spirit is the same word as was used of an engagement ring. And what is an engagement ring for? It is a definite demonstration of love and commitment; it is the first down-payment of the goods; it is a promise of better things to come. The Holy Spirit is God's irrevocable promise, his undeniable foretaste, of the riches that are to come. Through the creative influence of the Holy Spirit, we begin to see evidence of our glorious future, here and now! (Romans 8.14–18).

So the anonymous quotation, 'The future is not what it was', is not entirely true. Such are the chances and changes of life on earth, it is certainly the case that there are no guarantees about tomorrow. But the same cannot be said of those whose life is centred in God and whose future is tied up with his. Of such, Paul said this, 'Your life is hidden with Christ in God. When Christ who is your life is revealed, then you also will be revealed with him in glory' (Colossians 3.3–4). John added his own assurance: 'What we do know is this: when [Jesus] is revealed, we will be like him, for we will see him as he is' (1 John 3.2). The future, therefore, is Christ-shaped!

Action stations

But that doesn't mean that we are to 'pack our bags' and sign off, as it were, from the real world. On the contrary, we are to 'roll up our sleeves' and, with creativity and enthusiasm, live tomorrow's life today.

On the day when, as a twelve-year-old, I was told that I had been chosen to play for my school football team in the

Northern Ireland schools' cup final, I didn't sit at home and think, 'how lovely'. On the contrary, and to the annoyance of the neighbours, I kicked a ball up and down the street for a week before the game, every day anticipating the cup final and every day scoring the winning goal.

If our future is Christ-shaped, I believe that commits us to anticipate that future by living a Christ-shaped life in the present. The thought of that future, far from isolating us from the real world, will motivate us to get involved with that world and to challenge all that would diminish hope and destroy life within it. It will challenge us to walk alongside the vulnerable and powerless, the despised and rejected, the hurt and the forsaken, in order that we may serve as a beacon of hope for the immediate and long-term future. That is a practical and prayerful way of daily offering our future to God.

11
Death

Death can have its funny side – as I discovered one Tuesday morning five years ago. My telephone rang and a familiar voice from a church newspaper said, 'Roy, did you realize that your death has been listed on an internal document circulating around the House of Lords?' Wisely, she had checked with my local vicar that I was still in the land of the living before making the call, so she wasn't surprised to hear my voice. My response to her news was to roar with laughter; it was a rare privilege to assure her in the well-known words: 'Accounts of my demise are grossly exaggerated.'

I didn't, however, follow her suggestion to telephone the Palace of Westminster immediately. By not doing so, I hoped to avoid the possibility of a bizarre conversation through the switchboard at the House of Lords: 'Good morning. My name is Roy Williamson and I'm ringing to complain about the announcement of my death in the House notices.' I could imagine a prolonged and pregnant pause followed by a rather tentative, slightly embarrassed, enquiry, 'Where exactly are you ringing from, my Lord?'

It seemed wiser to send a gentle, handwritten, note to draw attention to the error and to advise that the announcement should be kept on file. It would be needed at a later date!

It comes to us all

My humorous advice to the Clerk of the House of Lords was not in the least facetious but entirely correct. The only certain thing about life is death. The only uncertain thing about death is its timing. Perhaps it is also true that we cannot make sense out of life until we have made sense out of death. That is not always as easy as it sounds; indeed, despite the fact that death is a universal experience, there often seems to be an inbuilt reluctance to think, let alone talk, about it. This may be understandable in the young, for whom death appears light years away, but for an 'oldie' like me, with one foot in the grave and the other on a banana skin, it would seem a little short-sighted. There is need, therefore, to grapple with the prospect of death, if only to get it in perspective, a task complicated by the variety of views about death.

Most of the major faiths have distinctive, and often differing, views about death and dying. But by far the greatest contrast, and the one most commonly expressed, lies between the secular and Christian view. To the secular mind, death is an ultimate disaster. It is to be avoided at all costs and to be deferred for as long as possible. There is a certain logic about such a view. If, as many believe, this life is the sum total of all there is, then death is indeed the ultimate disaster, the disintegration of all we are and have and ever hoped to be – and, perhaps, that doesn't bear thinking about. Death marks the end.

The Christian view is different. Death is something that comes to us all and, where the dying process makes it inevitable, we are to accept it. Where that is not the case, however, we should strive to prevent death, as the Good Samaritan did for the man mugged and left 'half-dead' on the Jericho road (Luke 10.30–37). For the Christian, therefore, though death is the outward sign of universal sinfulness – 'death spread to all because all have sinned' (Romans 5.12) – it is certainly not the ultimate disaster. St Paul makes clear that death is an essential preparation for resurrection. Our old body must die before we can be endowed with our new body, one that is appropriate to the new age. Our resurrection, like Christ's, is to eternal life and to a completely different mode of existence in that new age.

So, for the Christian, what matters most is not death, but a person's union with Christ. 'So if anyone is in Christ, there is a new creation: everything old has passed away; see, everything has become new!' (2 Corinthians 5.17).

The meaning of death was summed up succinctly by Dietrich Bonhoeffer, the German Lutheran theologian, before he was executed in Germany in 1945. 'Death', he said, 'is the supreme festival on the road to freedom.' It removes all restrictions and limitations. Death, far from being the end, marks the beginning of an inexhaustible adventure in the presence of God.

Humility in the face of mystery

Death may indeed be such a festival and adventure, but the process of dying, not only for the person concerned but also for loved ones watching, is not always a triumphant experience. Some are blessed with a 'beautiful' death. 'My bags are packed and I'm ready to go,' I have heard many elderly people say. Full of years, faith and serenity, their passing seems to be accomplished with a quiet dignity. For others, apart from the physical suffering, there is often the trauma of unfinished business, severed relationships, even feelings of guilt. For the bereaved there is, almost always, pain of loss and the need to rebuild broken lives.

In the light of these things, death must be treated with respect and humility. In the face of the mystery of death, there are times when a sense of awe is more appropriate than cries of victory. Some people, including Christians, are so eager to get to the Easter experience of joyful victory that they almost bypass the Good Friday experience of darkness and grief. In my limited experience I have discovered that triumphalism in the face of death is often followed by a period of dark depression.

I recall a rather painful episode of this nature while serving as a young curate. A friend and much respected senior priest died after a lengthy illness. Throughout the ordeal he maintained a wonderful witness of cheerfulness, courage and faith in the shadow of death, so that everyone coming to see him made a point of telling his wife how wonderful he was and sang his praises. His funeral was a triumphant affair with the note of victory sounding in every hymn and tribute. It was considered entirely fitting – and it was.

But for his wife who, while keeping a brave face, had been enduring a Good Friday experience of brokenness and desolation for months, the victorious nature of that service simply served to fill her with guilt at her inability to share in such 'triumphalism'. She hid her feelings well, but deep down she was angry with God, the church and even her late husband. In the weeks and months that followed, her sense of forsakenness increased as she began to search for a job, find another home, learn to drive a car and cope with a new and lonely lifestyle.

With the help of close friends, she eventually did move beyond Good Friday to Easter Day and was renewed in spirit and in faith. But it was a salutary reminder of the need for sensitivity and realism in the face of death – especially from those who are prone to sing songs of victory while distanced from its pain!

It is significant that Jesus Christ, the conqueror of both sin and death, wept at the graveside of his friend Lazarus (John 11.1–57). He ultimately raised the dead, but first he felt the pain and shared the sorrow of the bereaved, expressing grief and even anger at the destructive power of death. He knew that death was not the ultimate disaster but he also knew that, to Mary and Martha, it must have felt like it. He understood their jangling emotions, together with their disappointed hopes, bruised faith and genuine doubts about the future.

Faith in the face of doubt

It was into that confused, emotional and sorrowful situation at Bethany that Jesus introduced the need for faith. He didn't set aside nor despise these feelings of doubt or uncertainty; he understood them well and had wrestled with their pressures in the wilderness temptations (Matthew 4.1–11), and would do so again in the Garden of Gethsemane (Luke 22.39–46).

Instead, he brought these confused emotions into the larger context of faith. Fully appreciating the thoughts and feelings of his friends Mary and Martha, articulated in their wistful words, 'Lord, if you had been here, my brother would not have died,' he gently, but with persistence, helped the sorrowing sisters to refocus their feelings and their faith.

Doubt and uncertainty in the face of death is perfectly natural, and appropriate grief is usually essential, but they need to be brought within the larger context of faith's reality. Mary and Martha wanted to relegate that reality to the future and said of Lazarus, 'I know that he will rise again in the resurrection on the last day.' Jesus persists in helping them to see that his presence was that reality. As devout Jews their traditional belief in resurrection was to be, as it were, relocated in the person of Jesus and his resurrection. As Bishop Lesslie Newbigin wrote:

> Resurrection is no longer a mere doctrine: it has a living face and a name. Jesus is himself the presence of the life which is God's gift beyond death. To be bound to Jesus by faith is to share already now the life which is beyond death.

That, in essence, is the content of Jesus' words to Mary and Martha. 'I am the resurrection and the life. Those who believe in me, even though they die, will live, and everyone who lives and believes in me will never die. Do you believe this?' (John 11.25–26). Faith in and relationship with Jesus Christ is the source of the Christian's hope in the face of death.

This doesn't mean that we must be able to cross every 't' and dot every 'i' of the Nicene creed, for instance, before we can depart this life in peace. Heaven might be rather sparsely occupied if that were the case, but thank God it is not. My hope in the face of death lies in the depths of God's mercy and grace rather than the breadth of my theology, more in the richness of his love than the paucity of mine, more in the power of Christ's cross and resurrection, than my strength, or weakness, of faith.

Besides, at the point of death, our minds might be unable to focus on faith at all. It is at that point that the presence of family and friends and the ministry of the church is so important. I discovered this from personal experience when, two years after my ministry as a bishop began, I suffered a major heart attack and came very close to death. As the pain and darkness engulfed me, I found remarkable comfort not in a quick recollection of appropriate Bible verses – that was beyond me – but in the recollection of family love. A loving family had been my greatest joy, and I knew that the love of my children for their mother would continue to be her strength and support.

As I lay in a semi-conscious state in that London hospital, I was vaguely aware of an archbishop and one or two clerical colleagues standing at the foot of the bed. Wisely, they said nothing; it wouldn't have registered. Their presence, as representatives of the community of faith, was enough to remind me that I was surrounded and embraced by the love of God.

Later, as consciousness slowly returned, so did my sense of humour. I looked up and there, standing by my bedside, was a large man with a dark beard. He said, 'I'm the boss,' and for a fleeting moment, being a born optimist, I thought I was in heaven, but then he continued, 'The worst is over; all is well.' He was the specialist who, with sensitive pastoral care, had come to reassure me before he went off duty.

I have no doubt whatsoever that in the recollection of my family's love, the supportive presence of my colleagues and the medical skill of an unknown cardiologist, God had drawn near and walked with me, and, at least, showed me the entrance to the valley of the shadow of death.

The last offering

For many, however, the greatest area of uncertainty is not the entrance to but the exit from the valley of the shadow of death. What lies immediately on the other side of death?

Attempts to answer this question specifically and in detail are likely to be misleading. The Bible often uses picture language about the after-life, for instance in the parable of the rich man and Lazarus (Luke 16.19–31), but we must be careful in pressing the detail lest, like some, we develop a morbid interest in the furniture of heaven or the temperature of hell. Of much greater importance is what God has done for us in Christ.

Christians believe that God, in Christ, has entered into the reality of our death and overcome it. Christ's resurrection has radical implications for us. 'Because I live, you also will live,' he promised (John 14.19). His resurrection marked the end of the old life lived in the shadow of death, and the beginning of the new life lived in the light of eternity. The gift of his Holy Spirit means that we share in that new life.

Nevertheless, we are aware that evil still exists in God's world and we await its ultimate defeat. We recognize that though we have experienced the forgiveness of God, we still await transformation into the holy people he intends us to be. We haven't yet arrived but we 'press on towards the goal for the prize of the heavenly call of God in Christ Jesus' (Philippians 3.14). And though Christ has come to make all things new, we know that the healing of creation will only be complete when he returns and brings in the fullness of the kingdom. 'Creation awaits with eager longing for the revealing of the children of God' (Romans 8.19). So, as Christians, we accept that we live 'in between times', between what has been called the 'now' and the 'not yet'. We are people on the way.

That is also true of those who have died in Christ. They too are people on the way. They too await the coming of the kingdom in its fullness, the resurrection of their body and transformation into the likeness of Christ. They are with Christ on the way

But what does it mean for the dead to be 'with Christ'? Paul was convinced it was great gain. 'For to me, living is Christ and dying is gain... my desire is to depart and be with Christ, for that is far better' (Philippians 1.21, 23). He emphasized the same point in his letter to the Christians at Corinth: 'We would rather be away from the body and at home with the Lord' (2 Corinthians 5.8). As far as he was concerned, death would not break our union with Christ but establish it for ever, a conviction that formed the conclusion of his great chapter on Christian hope, so often read at funeral services:

> I am convinced that neither death nor life, nor angels nor rulers, nor things present, nor things to come, nor powers, nor height, nor depth, nor anything else in all creation, will be able to separate us from the love of God in Christ Jesus our Lord.
>
> (Romans 8.38–39)

Thus in life and in death, we are held within the same circle of God's love. In death we may move to the other half of that circle, where our experience of time may be different from those who are still alive, but the Spirit, given to us in life, will sustain us through death. The living and the dead in Christ form a common community, bound together in hope, waiting and longing for the fulfilment of God's promises for them to share in a new heaven and new earth. It is true, both for the living and the dead in Christ, that it has not yet been revealed what we will be. But when Christ is revealed, we, and they, will see him as he is and be like him (1 John 3.3). We shall also see one another as God intended us to be.

So death, our last offering to God, will lead us into the glory of his presence and the fullness of his kingdom.

12
Life

When I was a young boy we called it the 'Haunted House'. It was a massive Victorian building, standing in the middle of a large overgrown garden and surrounded by a high stone wall, on the top of which were coils of barbed wire and a warning notice: 'Keep out'. Such was the vivid imagination of my playmates and me that we projected all kinds of fantasies on to the house and its occupants. We saw mysterious lights, heard weird sounds and had mental pictures of headless figures appearing at midnight and dastardly deeds being done when the moon was full. We didn't mind walking past it during the day. At night we gave it a wide berth!

As we grew older, we had to revise our opinions. The house wasn't haunted. The owner had simply turned it into a forbidding fortress and defended it, as it were, against all visitors. Selfishly, he didn't want to open it to anyone else. All the amenities of that Victorian house, the potential of its spacious garden and the personalities of its hidden occupants, seemed to be imprisoned within that high stone wall. There was no evidence of sharing in any way with the local community.

It was not a haunted house, but it gave every indication of being a sad house. Over the years I watched its neglect and deterioration until, finally, it was demolished and the site was used to create a beautiful sheltered housing complex for the elderly.

A gift to be shared

On a recent visit to my homeland, that childhood memory suddenly sprang to life, and became remarkably apt, as I recalled some words of Henri Nouwen, regarding life. That respected and perceptive writer on spirituality said, 'Much violence is based on the illusion that life is a property to be defended and not a gift to be shared' (Ward and Wild, 1997).

Whether we see life as an accident, as some have described it, a cabaret, as Liza Minnelli declared it to be, a passing mist, as James has compared it to (James 4.14), or one of the many other descriptions people give to it, Nouwen's penetrating words are worthy of recollection and resolve at the beginning of each new day. Whatever our view of the origin or purpose of life, most would agree that it is not meant to be lived in isolation. Its beauty is not to be disfigured by a selfish attitude that unmistakably says to all and sundry, 'Keep out'. Its potential is not to be diminished by withdrawal from creative contact with other people.

Christians believe that life is the gift of God and that the rich and unique endowment, in terms of character and personality, given to each of us, will flourish best if we share it with others. And God, by personal example, has shown us the way to do it.

The God whom Christians worship has been revealed as Father, Son and Holy Spirit, three persons in one God. It is often referred to as the 'mystery' of the Holy Trinity, mainly because of the perfect relationship that exists between the three persons. Sharing rather than selfishness is the essence of that relationship. Giving and receiving of selfless love is at the heart of it.

Difficult though it may be to grasp, God is a communion of persons bound together in mutual giving and receiving. The self-giving love expressed between the persons of the Trinity is the creative force from which all things spring. Not surprisingly, therefore, human beings find fulfilment, and most clearly reveal that they are made in God's image, when they relate to one another in mutual love and self-giving.

That is God's way. From beginning to end the Bible is informed by a vision of human nature in which relatedness is fundamental. No person lives to himself or herself. That is why at the core of humanity there stands the covenant of the family. We were created to relate to one another in love. That is the way that leads to well-being for the whole of humankind, not only for those who are committed to faith in God but also for those who are not.

Pamela, for instance, was not a committed Christian. Occasionally she would appear in church for a special festival, but normally she was out and about in the community relating to people with special needs. The unsolicited view of that community was that she 'lived for others'. She loved people and her heart and home was open to them, though at times some took advantage of her kindness. Pamela's view was that she received more than she was able to give, and had grown as a person through sharing her life so openly with others.

Lindsey, on the other hand, was slightly more cautious in relating to people. By temperament she was a private person and somewhat hesitant about putting herself forward in helping others; besides, she had her own family to look after. But her faith was deep and her love for God found expression in her love for her neighbours. Mothers with young children found her to be a constant source of encouragement, inspiration and practical help. The friendships she formed were meaningful, and although she wasn't as well-known as Pamela within her local community, her quiet influence was greatly respected.

Lindsey and Pamela were different in character and outlook but, unconsciously, they held a common conviction that life was not a piece of private property to be defended against intruders, but a gift to be shared with others.

Life is for living

Lindsey and Pamela held another conviction in common, namely that life was for living. They had a positive view of life and, though their temperaments were different, they affirmed each new day and whatever lay ahead were determined to make the most of it. They might have had a slight difference of opinion about the first half of the well-known verse from the Psalms, but they would have heartily agreed with the second half – 'This is the day that the LORD has made; let us rejoice and be glad in it' (Psalm 118.24).

But while all may agree with them that life must be lived with a positive attitude, not everyone seems able or willing to follow their example. Cynicism and fear are but two of several attitudes that can negate the joy of living.

Alec, a small cockney man, was a rather painful, if humorous, example of the former. For years we met each morning at 7.30 as we walked our dogs on Tooting Bec Common. Every day he would greet me with the same words, 'Morning, mate. Ain't it bloomin' awful weather?' There was a seven-day period at the beginning of one summer when it was raining each morning. As we met, with the rain pouring from us and our dogs, Alec growled his familiar refrain with increasing intensity, 'Morning, mate. Ain't it bloomin' awful weather?'

On the eighth morning there was no rain. The sun had risen early, the sky was blue, the air warm and, as Alec and I approached each other, I wondered how he was going to cope with the change in the weather. I needn't have worried. 'Morning, mate,' he said, 'Wasn't it bloomin' awful weather yesterday?'!

I couldn't get home quick enough to tell the story over breakfast – though we could hardly eat for laughing. But behind the laughter, there was a very serious and depressing fact to be grasped. Alec's comment about the weather was symptomatic of his whole view of life, as I had discovered over the months. He was caught up in the culture of complaint that has entrapped so many. He was more ready to criticize than commend, to complain than express gratitude. Life was viewed through lenses of cynicism, pessimism and despair. He didn't believe that every cloud had a silver lining, but that every silver lining had a dirty great cloud in the middle! Like that old Victorian house in my homeland, there was an air of sadness, loneliness and hopelessness about Alec. Life was something to be grumbled at rather than grasped with joy and lived to the full.

Thankfully, not all are like Alec. Many are like Norman. He had every reason to be negative about life, for on the surface it hadn't treated him very well. His wife died just before he retired, and he lived alone in a flat on a large and socially deprived housing estate. But Norman shone like a beacon within that community. He could have closed his door, his mind, and his heart to life. Instead, he felt he owed it to his late wife, Ada, to make a positive contribution to life. He could have gone to live with his son in leafy Surrey, but chose to remain in south London. He enjoyed his trips to Surrey to play with his grandchildren, and was 'over the moon' when they came to visit him and he could take them to see 'the changing of the guard at Buckingham Palace' or watch Tower Bridge open up as ships passed through.

But most of his time was spent 'negating the negative' in his immediate environment. He was a key member of the tenants' association and kept an eye on the elderly and lonely in his particular block. He organized outings to Clacton, Brighton and Paris, and was always on hand to change washers on leaking taps and do the shopping for those with creaking limbs. Norman gave the impression that he couldn't get enough of life and, despite his advancing years, lived it with enthusiasm.

A journey of discovery

Alec saw life as a daily chore without purpose or direction. Norman, whose life had a religious dimension, saw it as a journey, with exciting possibilities of new experiences as well as its share of setbacks and sorrows. But then, Norman had that kind of temperament; he was a born optimist. There are many others who, even though sharing his religious convictions, would be more pessimistic than he. It is not that they are unbelieving or doubtful; they are just temperamentally fearful. On any journey they would be anxious about the mechanics of it; would they miss the train, would the plane crash, would the car break down?

But, whatever our temperament, we know that life, like every other journey, will have its twists and turns. There will be periods of calm and there will be times of storm, occasions when we walk through sunshine one minute and shadow the next. The detours, diversions and traffic jams we experience daily on our roads all have their equivalent in our journey through life and can produce the same level of frustration and uncertainty. Sometimes we are forced to turn back before we can move forward, to accept reversals and failures, disappointments and setbacks, before we can make progress. At other times, perhaps because of failing health, reduced circumstances or family crises, we feel our life has 'run into the sand', with no possibility of progress. And, just occasionally, we lose the way and need to ask for help.

Such things are commonplace. They are part and parcel of the journey. The things that happen to us in life are clearly important, but even more important, and perhaps ultimately more determinant, is our reaction to them. That is as true of triumphs as it is of tragedies, of small matters as it is of large. If we are able to view them as the raw material from which our characters are formed, then we can use them as building blocks rather than stumbling blocks.

However, a positive view like that is not always possible in the short term. It is true, as Søren Kierkegaard, the Danish philosopher and theologian, has reminded us, that 'Life is lived looking forward... but understood looking backward.' He is absolutely right. It is hard to understand when you are being overwhelmed by the sheer immensity of events – especially if they are tragic events. It is hard to think straight when, perhaps, you are scared stiff.

Those are the times when we need to ask for help and not be too proud to do so. If life is a gift to be shared, then that must mean the whole of life, including the failures as well as the successes, the sorrows as well as the joys. Besides, there are many sensitive and compassionate people around who are willing to share their life and experience, either by offering us practical help, or simply walking alongside us in our trouble, until we are able to rebuild our own lives again.

Abundant life

But whether our view of life is negative or positive or, depending on temperament and circumstances, somewhere in between, we must not ignore the amazing words of Jesus, when he described the purpose of his coming into the world: 'I came that they may have life, and have it abundantly' (John 10.10).

As always when reading the Bible, the context is important. In the form of a parable, Jesus had been drawing a comparison between the behaviour of those who are hired to look after sheep and himself as the good shepherd. Not only do the hirelings have no love for the sheep, they also put them in danger by deserting them, exposing them to wolves and thieves and possible death. By contrast Jesus, as the good shepherd, loves his sheep, refuses to leave them unprotected and is prepared to give his life for them.

In reality, Jesus was contrasting the behaviour of the religious leaders of Israel with his own purposes for the people of Israel. They had betrayed their trust by placing their own interests before those of the people in their care. They were saving their own lives at the expense of others. Jesus, on the other hand, was prepared to give his own life in order that others may have life 'abundantly'. He made the same point in what is perhaps the best known verse of scripture and the most superb summary of the entire Christian gospel: 'For God so loved the world that he gave his only Son, so that everyone who believes in him may not perish but may have eternal life' (John 3.16).

The purpose of Christ's coming into the world was, through his death and resurrection, to provide life that had something of the quality of God's own life about it. That is what the word life means in this context. It is a quality of life above and beyond that which is currently contained within our mortal bodies and enclosed within our material world. It is a quality of life that death cannot destroy, because it belongs to the new age and new order that Christ inaugurated through his death and resurrection. Paul described it in these terms: 'If anyone is in Christ, there is a new creation: everything old has passed away; see, everything has become new!' (2 Corinthians 5.17). In other words, this 'abundant life', which had the quality of eternity about it, begins now, in time, when we are drawn by God's love into Christ.

The life of God

This life, which begins in the here and now and which death cannot destroy, is guaranteed by the presence of God's Holy Spirit that he has given to us. 'When we cry, "Abba! Father!", it is that very Spirit bearing witness with our spirit that we are children of God, and if children, then heirs, heirs of God and joint heirs with Christ' (Romans 8.15). The Holy Spirit is the breath – the life – of God, given to us. We share the life of God. This truth was beautifully expressed by Austin Farrer, when he wrote,

> The gift of the Holy Spirit closes the last gap between the life of God and ours... When we allow the love of God to move in us, we can no longer distinguish ours and his; he becomes us, he lives in us. It is the first fruit of the Holy Spirit, the beginning of our being made divine.
> (Ward and Wild, 1997)

This brings us back to where we began this chapter, with the reminder that the God whom Christians worship is a communion of persons who exist in a relationship of perfect mutuality. There is a rhythm of self-giving life and love eternally flowing between them. It would be a great mistake, however, to see the persons of the Trinity as a kind of holy huddle, or divine admiration society. Nothing could be further from the truth.

The circle of the Trinity, if I may put it like that, is not a closed circle. It is open to us. The love of God the Father moved outwards in creation and was made visible to us through the grace of his Son, our Lord Jesus Christ, as he came to live among us. That same love is poured into our hearts by his Holy Spirit (Romans 5.5). The amazing truth about all this is that God invites us to share and be caught up in the relationships of the Father, the Son and the Holy Spirit. Thus God shares with us his love and his life. We become 'participants in the divine nature' (2 Peter 1.4).

Such amazing grace, far from filling us with elitist pride, should surround us with deep humility, and inspire us to offer our life daily to God, that in the midst of the complexities of modern day living we may reveal something of his life to a needy and incredulous world.

Epilogue

My study is so small that I can sit in the middle of it and touch all four walls. I am surrounded by books, Christian symbols and photographs of places and people that have significance in my life and ministry. But there is one unique feature – a small alabaster plaque with a pair of open hands engraved on it.

The plaque was a birthday gift from my youngest grandchild. He was only eighteen months old at the time and wanted to send his grandfather a birthday card but, of course, he couldn't write his signature. However, a little creative thinking and imaginative action on his mother's part solved the problem, and on my birthday the treasured plaque arrived. It now hangs beside the small wooden cross that marks the corner where I sit to say my prayers.

In some respects the hands of my grandson, with their palms turned upward, have been the inspiration for this little book. In the preceding chapters I have not outlined a detailed methodology of prayer, being more concerned with holding a vision in which the whole of life can become a prayer offered daily to God. Every day, in some shape or form, the faculties, relationships and rhythms of life that form the content of the book impact upon our lives and often determine the kind of people we are. How important it is, therefore, that we acknowledge God as the creator and sustainer of life and recall that our lives are lived before him.

Open hands with palms turned upward are symbolic of a readiness to offer to God all that we have, and are, and hope to be. They are also a symbol of our willingness to receive from him all that he wishes to give us. It is this pattern of giving and receiving, receiving and giving, that finds perfect expression among the persons of the Trinity, that gives life its meaning and significance.

It is my hope that the simple theme I have tried to pursue in these pages may provide a framework that will contribute to that meaning and significance, by bringing a sense of integration and wholeness to our lives in a beautiful, if complex and fragmented, world.

Anthology of Prayers

Hands

Lord,
I place my hands in yours,
that the work you have given me to do this day
  may be done with creativity and
    singleness of mind;
and that through them, your love and practical
  compassion
  may be expressed to those who are in need.

*

Jesus' hands were kind hands, doing good to all,
healing pain and sickness, blessing children small;
washing weary feet, and saving those who fall;
Jesus' hands were kind hands, doing good to all.

Take my hands, Lord Jesus, let them work for you,
make them strong and gentle, kind in all I do;
let me watch you, Jesus, till I'm gentle too,
till my hands are kind hands, quick to work for you.

Margaret Cropper

Eyes

Teach me, my God and King,
  In all things thee to see;
And what I do in anything
  To do it as for thee!

A man that looks on glass,
  On it may stay his eye;
Or if he pleaseth, through it pass,
  and then the heaven espy.

George Herbert

Open our eyes, O Lord,
to the signs of encouragement all around us
  in the lives of ordinary people.
We thank you for those whose courage and
  fortitude inspire us;
and pray for strength to stand firm in our own
  times of adversity.

Mouth

God be in my mouth and in my speaking.
Save me from making foolish talk,
  using hurtful words,
  or uttering false promises.
Give me courage to say what I mean
  and the honesty to mean what I say.
Help me always to speak with kindness
  and may the things I say encourage
    and enrich the lives of others.
God be in my mouth and in my speaking.

*

Let the words of my mouth and the
  meditation of my heart
    be acceptable to you,
      O Lord, my rock and my redeemer.

Psalm 19.14

O Jesus, Son of God, who was silent before Pilate, do not let us wag our tongues without thinking of what we are to say and how to say it.

Irish Gaelic

Heart

Lord,
I offer you my heart this day.
Pour into it the fullness of your love,
that it may overflow
　into the lives of others;
bringing hope to the despairing,
　inspiration to those who would follow you
　and light to all who have lost the way.
Lord, keep my heart tender,
　that others might find me easy to deal with
　and I might receive the creative imprint
　　of your touch.

*

O thou who camest from above,
The pure celestial fire to impart,
Kindle a flame of sacred love
On the mean altar of my heart.

There let it for thy glory burn
With inextinguishable blaze,
And trembling to its source return
In humble prayer, and fervent praise.

Charles Wesley

Mind

God our Father,
you are the source of wisdom
  and understanding,
illuminate our minds by your Holy Spirit,
that we may understand your truth
  and respond to it with reverence,
    humility and joy.

May the mind of Christ my Saviour
  live in me from day to day,
by his love and power controlling
  all I do and say.

Kati B. Wilkinson

Holy Spirit, think through me
till your ideas are my ideas.

Amy Carmichael

Will

Father, not my will but your will be done.

Luke 22.42 (Good News Bible)

Lord, thou knowest what I want,
if it be thy will that I have it;
and if it be not thy will,
good Lord, do not be displeased,
for I want nothing which you do not want.

Julian of Norwich

Into your hands, merciful Lord, we commend ourselves for this day; may we be aware of your presence until its end; remind us that in whatever good we do we are serving you; make us

careful and watchful, so that in everything we may discern
your will, and, knowing it, may gladly obey, to the honour and
glory of your name; through Jesus Christ our Lord.

Gelasian Sacramentary

Friends, neighbours, enemies

Heavenly Father,
look in love on all our friends and neighbours.
Keep them from harm,
deepen our friendship with them
and may we grow in love for you,
our Saviour and friend.

Michael Botting

Lord Jesus Christ,
you loved and prayed for your enemies.
Give us grace so to follow your example
that we and they may come to the place of
  reconciliation and peace.

*

I saw a stranger today
I put food for him in the eating-place
And drink in the drinking-place
And music in the listening-place.
In the Holy Name of the Trinity
He blessed myself and my house
My goods and my family.
And the lark said in her warble
Often, often, often
Goes Christ in the stranger's guise
O, oft and oft and oft,
Goes Christ in the stranger's guise.

A rune of hospitality

Past

God, our Father,
Lord of all the earth and all time,
  we give you thanks for your faithfulness
    in past years;
  for your patience with our mistakes,
  for your mercy in times of folly,
  for your forgiveness of our sin,
  and for your love that has never ceased.
Set us free from those things in our past
  that threaten to paralyse our life
  in the present and
  give us grace to grow in truth and holiness,
    through Jesus Christ our redeemer.

*

O Lamb of God,
That takest away the sins of the world,
Grant us thy peace.

Book of Common Prayer

Lord Jesus Christ, Son of God,
have mercy on me, a sinner.

Eastern Orthodox

Present

This is the day that the LORD has
  made;
let us rejoice and be glad in it.

Psalm 118.24

Lord Jesus Christ,
alive and at large in the world,
help me to follow and find you there today,
　in the places where I work,
　　meet people,
　　spend money,
　　and make plans.
Take me as a disciple of your kingdom,
　to see through your eyes,
　and hear the questions you are asking,
　to welcome all people with your trust and truth,
and to change the things that contradict God's love,
　　by the power of the cross
and the freedom of your Spirit. Amen.

John V Taylor, former Bishop of Winchester

Future

Lord Jesus Christ,
you are the same yesterday and today
　and for ever.
I place myself in your hands.
My future lies in yours.

*

Thy way not mine, O Lord,
However dark it be;
Lead me by thine own hand,
Choose out the path for me.
Smooth let it be or rough,
It will be still the best;
Winding or straight, it leads
Right onward to thy rest.
Choose thou for me my friends,
My sickness or my health;
Choose thou my cares for me,

My poverty or wealth.
Not mine, not mine the choice
In things or great or small;
Be thou my guide, my strength,
My wisdom, and my all.

Horatius Bonar

Death

O God, who brought us to birth,
and in whose arms we die,
in our grief and shock,
contain and comfort us;
embrace us with your love,
give us hope in our confusion,
and grace to let go into new life,
through Jesus Christ.

Janet Morley

Bring us, O Lord God, at our last awakening into the house and gate of heaven, to enter into that gate and dwell in that house, where there shall be no darkness nor dazzling, but one equal light; no noise nor silence, but one equal music; no fears nor hopes, but one equal possession; no ends nor beginnings, but one equal eternity; in the habitation of thy glory and dominion world without end.

John Donne

O Lord, you have made us very small, and we bring our years to an end like a tale that is told; help us to remember that beyond our brief day is the eternity of your love.

Reinhold Niebuhr

Life

Father, hear the prayer we offer:
 Not for ease that prayer shall be,
But for strength that we may ever
 Live our lives courageously.

Maria Willis

Father of all mercies,
we are thankful for our creation
and for the gift of life
 which we hold in trust from you.
Teach us to value it and use it to the full.
Help us to guard against all that would
 diminish it and to pursue those things that will
 enable it to flourish,
that we may bring glory to your name.
 faithfully serve your church
  and the good of all people.

*

Dear God, be good to me;
The sea is wide,
And my boat is small.

*Breton fishermen's
prayer*

General

God be in my head, and in my understanding;
God be in my eyes, and in my looking;
God be in my mouth, and in my speaking;
God be in my heart, and in my thinking;
God be at my end, and at my departing.

Sarum Primer

Lord Jesus,
I give thee my hands to do thy work.
I give thee my feet to go thy ways.
I give thee my eyes to see as thou seest.
I give thee my tongue to speak thy words.
I give thee my mind that thou mayest think in me.
I give thee my spirit that thou mayest pray in me.
Above all, I give thee my heart that thou
　mayest love in me thy Father and all mankind.
I give thee my whole self that thou mayest
　grow in me.
So that it is thee, Lord Jesus, who lives and
　works and prays in me.

Lancelot Andrewes

Lord,
　Take our hands and work with them;
　Take our lips and speak through them;
　Take our minds and think with them;
　Take our hearts and set them on fire with love
　　for you and all creation.

*

I place my hands in yours Lord
I place my hands in yours

I place my will in yours Lord
I place my will in yours

I place my days in yours Lord
I place my days in yours

I place my thoughts in yours Lord
I place my thoughts in yours

I place my heart in yours Lord
I place my heart in yours

I place my life in yours Lord
I place my life in yours

David Adam

Christ be with me, Christ within me,
Christ behind me, Christ before me,
Christ beside me, Christ to win me,
Christ to comfort and restore me,
Christ beneath me, Christ above me,
Christ in quiet, Christ in danger,
Christ in hearts of all that love me,
Christ in mouth of friend and stranger.

St Patrick

Teach me, O God to use all the circumstances of my life today that they may bring forth in me the fruits of holiness rather than the fruits of sin.
    Let me use disappointments as material for patience:
    Let me use success as material for thankfulness:
    Let me use suspense as material for perseverance:
    Let me use danger as material for courage:
    Let me use reproach as material for longsuffering:
    Let me use praise as material for humility:
    Let me use pleasure as material for temperance:
    Let me use pains as material for endurance.

John Baillie

References

Bancroft, Charity Lees, hymn 169 in *Sing Glory*, Kevin Mayhew, 1999.

Blythe, Robert, *The View in Winter*, Allen Lane, 1979.

Bonhoeffer, Dietrich, *Letters and Papers from Prison*, SCM Press, 1971, p. 163.

Brueggemann, Walter, *Prophetic Imagination*, Fortress Press, 1978, p. 11.

Küng, Hans, *On Being a Christian*, Collins, 1997, p. 231.

Newbigin, Lesslie, *The Light Has Come*, Eerdmans, 1982, p. 142.

Saint-Exupéry, Antoine de, *The Little Prince*, trans. Katherine Woods, Heinemann, 1997.

Stott, J. R. W., *The Message of the Sermon on the Mount*, IVP, 1978, p. 155.

Ward, Hannah, and Wild, Jennifer (eds), *Christian Quotation Collection*, Lion, 1997.

Wodehouse, P. G., *The Code of the Woosters*, Penguin Classics, 2001.